Emory Campbell walking down dirt roads in Bay Gall on Hilton Head Island, South Carolina

Gullah Cultural Legacies

A Synopsis of Gullah Traditions, Customary Beliefs, Artforms and Speech on Hilton Head Island and Vicinal Sea Islands in South Carolina and Georgia

Emory S. Campbell

Introduction by Ayoka Campbell

Gullah Heritage Consulting Services

ISBN 0-9700173-1-6

Published in the United States of America.

Second Edition

Printed in United States of America

Contents

Dedicated to the

Memory of my
Grandparents, Perry and Rosa Williams
Solomon and Julia Campbell
And to the memory of my parents
Reginald and Sarah Campbell
And to my caring wife, Emma
And children, Ochieng and Ayoka
And to
Penn Center, one of the
Most important repositories
Of Gullah Cultural Legacies in the nation.

About This Book

This book contains significant cultural words and terms of the Gullah Culture. It is an attempt to promote a better understanding of past traditions and present day practices in preventing permanent loss of memory of those terms that are truly Gullah. Most of the terms are currently used in the everyday vocabulary of Gullah speakers, while others have fallen into disuse but have been recalled for inclusion in this work. The content of this book is based entirely on my experience of growing up Gullah on Hilton Head Island in the mid 20th century before the Island was connected by a bridge to the mainland.

Life on Hilton Head Island between the 1860's and the 1960's was a unique, cultural experience when compared to mainland lifestyle during the same period. The culture that thrived on Hilton Head and other Coastal Islands in the region had its beginning on the West Coast of Africa. Before being imported to the Sea Islands during the despicable slave trade period between the 1500's and early 1800's, West Africans not only survived, they thrived – spiritually, intellectually, and physically– mainly because family members and families bonded to one another. After slavery, a close- knit community evolved with these basic qualities already in place drawing on each separately and collectively as time moved from period to period.

Throughout the history of Gullah culture, place has been important – whether it was the huge oak tree in the forest where a "young *soul*" went to meditate while *seeking* or the *landing* where a fisherman kept his or her *bateau* so it would float appropriately when the tide was right to "go *casting*."

The Gullah language, perhaps more than any other cultural asset, has allowed Gullah people to remain one big family. It has kept us intellectual, esoteric and protected. Yet it has been so attractive to others that the entire culture has reached the larger world.

Like with all cultures, food grounds the Gullah culture. Saltwater rice-eating *Geechees* is the term commonly used among Black people to describe their African *kins* who live along the saltwater coast. The key word here is rice, a most enjoyable staple in the daily diet of every traditional Gullah family. The fact that West Africans had been growing and preparing delicious rice dishes five thousand years before the slave trade began is not lost on our love of rice dishes. A *mulatto* rice *Pilau* with freshly fried fish; *swimp* & okra and matos (*gumbo*); peas and rice; sweet *tater*; and watermelon would all but confirm the Gullah legacy.

Our spirituality has always been secured by an abiding faith in varied historic beliefs that may transcend religions and denominations. Some Gullah people on occasions combine Christian beliefs with those of ancient Africa to satisfy their spiritual need. For example, one might combine meditation at the *mourning bench* with a hand from a witch doctor to meet one's worldly need.

Art forms have always been critical to the survival of Gullah people. A *bateau* and a *cast net* have been used for hundreds of years to gather food from creeks and rivers when access to natural resources was truly available to everyone. Also, a *sweet grass basket* has been a valuable houseware, which is today a much- desired commemorative art.

Like most cultures, the Gullah culture has not changed solely on its own terms. Most changes have been forced on it through land use and other mainstream policies despite resistance and the obvious inability for various reasons to adapt to the new culture. These policies are often the result of policy makers not understanding the culture and in some cases unwilling to learn.

WHAT IS GULLAH?

In a brief word **Gullah** is a culture comprising a system of beliefs, customs, artforms, foodways, and language practiced among descendants of West Africans who settled along the coasts of North Carolina, South Carolina, Georgia and Florida from slavery period to present. The culture is a carry-over from that which thrives in parts of West Africa. Today, it is estimated by some that more than a quarter million people fit the definition of Gullah in a defined region. The area includes nearly 100 barrier islands from Sapelo, Georgia, southward to Daufuskie, Hilton Head, and Johns Island northward.

Although curiosity of the origin of the word Gullah has produced several commentaries, perhaps the most commonly accepted linkage is to Angola. It is widely believed that the regularity of enslaved Angolans arriving at various coastal ports gave rise to the term "Gola Negroes" which later became Gullah.

But many, particularly African Americans, use the term Geechee to describe this unique culture. It is commonly accepted that enslaved West Africans were smuggled into Georgia waterways settling along the Ogeechee River in South Georgia. Thus the term Geechee is used almost exclusively among African Americans when referring to Blacks who live in coastal South Carolina and Georgia.

Until the last half of the 20th Century the Coastal communities of South Carolina and Georgia were populated almost entirely by African Americans. The harsh, humid climate and accompanying Malaria disease deterred white occupancy during slavery, thus allowing for maintaining ethnic purity and development of a hybrid West African culture that would come to be known as Gullah. This provincial existence largely contributed to the mystique that has always been perceived by those who are not connected to the culture.

In his *Souls of Black Folks*, W.E.B. DuBois describes the first time the Yankees, who arrived at the Sea Islands at the beginning of the Civil War, met the Africans. DuBois states that these troops and volunteers had absolutely not even an inkling of what they were hearing in speech and songs or seeing in the unique dark facial features. Yet these unique people were the freshest evidence of Africans held in bondage for which the conquest was being waged.

These same African people became the focus of the nation early in the Civil War on the issue of their ability to live as free people. Known to historians as the Port Royal Experiment, the Sea Island Africans affirmed three questions that were the essence of the issue: (1) Would the Africans fight for their freedom? The first Black regiment in the South was organized in the Port Royal area; (2) Can they become educated? One of the first schools for the previously enslaved was organized as Penn School and produced a number of learned young Gullahs; (3) Could the Africans become landowners? By the end of 1862, a substantial number of those formerly enslaved had purchased parcels of the plantations using earnings from labor rendered as contrabands to Northern businessmen who operated cotton plantations in the Union-occupied Sea Islands.

Thus the Gullah Culture began to evolve. For the next 100 years a culture would evolve in the islands that would reflect its West African ancestry.

PREFACE

I was nearly a half- century old when I realized that the culture in which I was born, Gullah, contains uniquely, rich folklore and a fascinating distinguished idiom. I realized that waterways and the Atlantic Ocean that encircled my native Hilton Head and other islands keeping us afar from mainstream America for many years had also kept our culture relatively pure. Our fellow African-Americans had known us as Geechees and scholars had known us as Gullahs. I suddenly realized that for the greater part of my life perhaps, I had been more African than American. But even more revealing was the fact that nearly a half million African-Americans who live along the coast of North Carolina, South Carolina, and Georgia were so distinguished.

The foods we ate, the songs we sang, the spirits we embraced, the noble families in which we were loved, and the language we spoke, I had taken all for granted. Through the years each of us had thought that our lifestyle was as American as lifestyles elsewhere. But as people from elsewhere came to the islands and as some of us left and stayed in parts of the mainland, we got inklings that something about "we islanders" was different. Sensing that being different culturally presented difficulty in assimilating with mainlanders, most of us would take advantage of every chance to learn new folkways and abandon our own. We would adopt a new idiom and deny that our own ever existed. We made concerted efforts to become imitations of mainland Americans.

Those who migrated to Savannah became "citified." Those who migrated to New York, Boston, Philadelphia, and places north of the Mason and Dixon became instant Yankees, adapting to all features of the Yankee culture and perfect Yankee speech patterns.

As Europeans were settling the Sea Islands in the 16th and 17th centuries, West Africans, whence Gullah descended, enjoyed a beautiful culture of tightly knitted village life. They cultivated rice, okra, yams, benne, and gourd as normal crops. They weaved baskets, knitted nets, and made boats as a part of daily chores to sustain villages. And their language had no need for English words.

From the late 1600's until the mid 1800's a large number of these West Africans were enslaved and imported to the Sea Islands of South Carolina and Georgia to plantation systems, bringing their memories of family life, customs, food ways, folklore, language and pride. During this period, these West Africans made only necessary adjustments to their original lifestyle.

Such was the lifestyle of thousands of Africans when the Civil War began in 1861 engaging the islands of Hilton Head, Daufuskie, St. Helena, Sapelo, St. Simons, Wadmalaw, Johns, and others.

Although their very soul had been tempered by more than 200 years of chattel slavery, these Africans still believed in the legitimacy of their folkways, capabilities, and humanity. Sea Island slave plantation systems had always been predominantly occupied by Africans, which enabled them to redevelop their West African culture. Families remained noble and tightly knit; rice, yams and okra were favorite foods; women toted items on their heads; Bro rabbit and Bro fox folktales were popular entertainment; and a mixture of African and English words formed the language.

Hundreds of volunteers streamed to the Sea Islands after the Civil War began to establish schools so that these Africans would have a chance to blend into mainstream America. Subsequently, a number of schools were established. One of the most successful among them was Penn School on Saint Helena Island, whose benefactors were two women, Laura Towne and Ellen Murray both of Philadelphia. Although their benevolence was largely appreciated by those touched, Towne's and Murray's euro centric curricula essentially suppressed Africanisms among their students.

When my older siblings and other relatives would return after a full year at Penn School, there was no trace of their Gullah speech, although peas, sweet potatoes, and rice remained among their favorite foods. And just as we made efforts at home to change our hair and skin texture to become more "acceptable" to other Americans, Penn School was exhorting its students to "get cultured." The school was teaching them to look and act like European-Americans so that they would be accepted as mainstream Americans.

Despite extreme inconveniences owed to troubled waters, the absence of bridges to the mainland, oppressive hot summers and pestilent mosquitoes, there was sporadic pilgrimage to the various islands for various reasons. Family members from the mainland came to hunt and fish, attend weddings or funerals while scholars from colleges and universities came to examine and document various aspects of the Gullah culture.

Even though journeys to the islands were some times leisurely, careful planning and particular arrangements had to be made for transportation during hunting and fishing seasons. Of course, all resources were brought to bear for funerals and other emergencies that required mainlanders' travel to the islands and vice versa.

On the other hand, significant Africanisms among Gullah people have been retained, despite ridicule and efforts to change the Gullah people's natural lifestyles. The language and food have prevailed among many of us who refuse to be changed. My own high school and college experience is perhaps typical of the mockery most Gullah youth encounter about their dialect and food ways. During formal presentations in class I would try my best to change my accent, but during casual conversations, my Gullah would produce endless laughter and questions about my roots. The routine line of questions that often followed my sentences included- "Where are you from,

Daufuskie?, Africa? The West Indies? What's a *coota?* Say boat again." Of course, my love of sweet potatoes and rice were dead giveaways that I was indeed a "salt-water Geechee."

Eventually, I realized that my attempts to suppress my natural Gullah lifestyle were futile, but I would have never stopped trying if I had not become the Executive Director of the place that had successfully suppressed the language for many years. Then in the early 1980s, after becoming the Executive Director of Penn Center, I met two wonderful scholars, Joseph Holloway and Joseph Opala. These two scholars would help me make a personal connection to West Africa, which I could share with many others for years to come.

Introduction

"You are foreign aren't you?" the receptionist questioned, after my father bent his lean, 6' 4" frame over the counter and asked directions to the Admissions Office as I was seeking to enter Howard University. She had attempted to send us to the International Admissions Office. In expressing her sincere apology she said, "I thought I detected a foreign accent." Ever since that day I have appreciated the fact that my father is one of those unique African Americans who grew up on the isolated islands off the East Coast of the United States. We are widely known as Gullahs and more esoterically as Geechees. I have also realized that it is important that he records the history of these native islanders. Being constantly mistaken as one from the continent of Africa, confirms the fact that there is a true connection between Gullah people and Africans, who had never left the continent. We are descendants of enslaved people brought from Africa some 400 years ago, who have retained Africanisms in our speech, food ways, and daily ways of living.

Although my father has set out to briefly note Gullah terms that he used growing up on the island of Hilton Head in South Carolina, now one of the world's premier resorts, islanders in black Diasporas, around the globe may recognize these terms. I, as a younger islander, grasped these terms as I grew up some 30 years after my father's childhood, because the island still had remnants of the lifestyle my father experienced in the 1940s. Just as he had done, years later, I would stand on the same creek shore, throwing out a string line, with the same kind of bait, tied with a string on a small wooden twig to catch crabs. I would experience the same "Gullah" world. Living in this tribe-like world, with the melodic sounds of a language of our native African tongue a world away, I would join my brother and cousins encircling the big black pot over a wood fueled fire as dozens of crabs we caught boiled to a Gullah delicacy. And my recent memory takes me to our garden where we would pluck fresh green corn from the stock and pick a juicy watermelon from the vine to complete the feast in Sister's (grandmother) yard.

My father would always talk to me in two languages – one African and one American. "Ye yent"!! is what he would exclaim whenever I made what seemed to him to be an unbelievable statement. After my astonished reaction to this and other Gullah terms he would translate them to English for me. "Ye yent" means "Is that true" in English.

Because over time, these precious words, phrases, and historic objects could dwindle away with the fading native, Gullah speakers, my father has been encouraged to preserve these relics of Gullah cultural heritage. The terms in this book capture a nature of life very unique to the Sea Islands off the South Eastern Coast of the United States.

But I am convinced that the rhythmic speech of these terms is deeply rooted in Africa. While listening to a man from Liberia, Africa speaking on the Howard University radio station, I was surprised by how much he sounded like my father. All of my life, I had heard him, his brothers and sisters, his mother, (intensive mainland schooling had virtually erased his father's Gullah speech pattern) and other native islanders of Hilton Head and surrounding islands speak the Gullah language—a mix of African and American words using an African grammar pattern.

Although I realized that they were speaking a different language, I could not always clearly recognize its pattern. However it was obvious to me that they generally understood each other. For example, I recall an elderly Gullah Deacon offering a prayer in church, and my cousin and I falling to the floor laughing under the pews, because none of his words were familiar to us. However, much to our surprise, most of the worshipers were nodding their heads with enthusiastic Amens.

Language is an important part of the culture, but the legacy of Gullah people is also rich with religious rituals, material culture such as sweet grass basket weaving, fishnet making, and food ways.

As a newspaper reporter and freelance researcher in my early professional life, this legacy became tangible to me. In an effort to record this history in the early 1990s, I visited different Hilton Head native islanders. Showing up one day unannounced, I watched through a sliding glass door, one of the Island's beloved elders, patiently knitting a fish net. He just sat in his living room knitting with no real concentration. It is an art he had learned at an early age. His wife who extolled her own knitting skills boasted that her husband was a prolific net maker. These nets now join many of the relics of Hilton Head Island.

But what intrigued me most were the religious rituals that were practiced until recent years past. My research took me to another elderly couple who proudly gave me details of their spiritual experience through dreams and meditations that were required while "seeking" to become a member of the church. Scholars have confirmed that dream interpretations and solitary meditations in the forest as these elders explained to me, are related to West African historic religious practices.

I was very lucky to have opportunities afforded me to draw specific details from those who were well grounded in our culture. And I found them to be proudly willing to share precious cultural anecdotes that boosted my own curiosity to find out more about myself.

Festivals and family reunions are other great sources where one gets tastes of this unique Gullah World. These joyous events feature fresh seafood dishes, basket weaving, Sea Island spirituals and more. As early as I can remember our family would attend the various festivals and Celebrations held on Islands in proximity to Hilton Head. We would attend them as far away northward in our own state at Wadmalaw and John's and southward in Georgia at Saint Simons and Sapelo.

At Daufuskie Day to which we traveled via an excursion boat in the early morning, just a few miles down river from Hilton Head, I looked forward to dining on the world's most delicious deviled crabs. The Georgia Sea Islands Festival at Saint Simons, the oldest of them all, featured the best of the thigh slapping Gospel quartets and the world's best tasting smoked mullets. I remember the first time ever riding in a Mule-drawn wagon and observing a bateau built at Penn Center Heritage Days Celebration. Riding in the parade and listening to Gullah folktales were also special treats. Of course the numerous rice dishes, the trademark of Gullah culture, is the center piece of all Gullah cultural celebrations

And I have always looked forward to our annual family reunions when I meet relatives for the first time. It does not matter how far apart we live or how distant the kinship we Gullahs cherish blood lineage. My Grandmother would be certain that I understood how my young 6th cousin in Boston or my elderly 8th cousin in California and I were connected. But as a child, listening to the family stories was the highlight of family reunions for me. Learning about the characteristics of family members whom had passed on made me feel proud. At one reunion I learned about how my seafaring great uncles regularly sailed self-made boats loaded with fish, watermelon and other goods, from Hilton Head, over treacherous waters, to trade at the market in Savannah.

However, home is where the heart is. Whenever one enters a Native Islander's home one finds that these rituals and items are not just something of the past, but still a part of their every day life, which are passed on from generation to generation.

We who are descendants of Gullah hold these relics dear forever. Home is where the culture will always strive. I now live in the Washington, D.C. area and my brother now lives in Houston, Texas. But if you walk into our houses any day, you may smell the seafood, hear our slight accent, and have a feeling of being on a continent some world away.

My father, along with other scholars, has had the opportunity to make the cultural linkage to Africa, continuously educating people about the connection between Gullahs and West Africans. Living the culture as he does, I believe he is well prepared to record terms that help one to see, feel, touch, hear, and smell Gullah culture. These terms will serve as a wonderful guide to understanding fundamental traditions of us Gullahs. And I am certain that those who are a part of the African Diaspora and others can sense the connections. It is my hope that this book will give you a peek into our world of often called "peculiar" people living mainly off the coast of the Carolinas and Georgia.

- Ayoka Campbell

A	Definition
After the bridge	Most Sea Islands histories are distinguished by periods before and after they are connected to the mainland by bridges. In Hilton Head Island vernacular, refers to the period beginning in May 1956 when Hilton Head was connected to the mainland for the first time in its history. Named for Governor James Burns, the "Burns Crossing," a draw bridge, tolled each car $1.25 each way initially before it became free passage two years later. The present fixed-span bridge replaced the Burns Crossing in 1982. Before the Bridge, transportation to the mainland from Hilton Head Island was provided by individuals rowing bateaux, or by sailboats. Two island businessmen later operated gasoline powered passenger ferryboats. Charlie Simmons was the first Gullah person to own a gasoline powered boat. Among the several boats he owned in succession were "the Edgar Hurst" and "the Alligator." Arthur Frazier owned "The Vernon." These men were licensed transporters who carried passengers and freight to and from Savannah. A government-sponsored boat liner operated between Beaufort and Savannah twice weekly between the 1940's and early 1950's carrying passengers and the U.S. mail.
Ansa	Answer. To reply Ex. I be ansa him
Ax	Ask – as pronounced by Gullah speakers. To Inquire *Ex. He ax me way de beach da.*

B	Definition
Backseat	The last seat in the praise house or church. The place assigned to members who violate church law or ethics. Community members were disciplined by church sanctions instead of the government legal system.
Basket name	The name given soon after birth usually because of circumstances surrounding birth while the baby is kept in a basket that was used as a bassinet, (i.e. One may be given the name of the day on which one was born or for the weather conditions as his/her basket name, (i.e., Sunday or Stormy)). An official name is registered with the governmental agency. Therefore Gullah people usually have two names although community members often know only their basket names.
Bateau	A small, flat bottom boat traditionally used in islands' creeks for gathering seafood. Bateaux were built by men in various neighborhoods often propelled by adults as well as by young children using oars that were often hand-made.
Beach Picnic	A traditional sponsored gathering on the beach (usually by a church) that took place once a year. Island families (adults and children) enjoyed hotdogs, potato salad, fried chicken, watermelon, corn on the cob, etc. Children and adults were well dressed in their "Sunday go to meeting clothes." Seldom did anyone go bathing.

B	Definition
Before the Bridge	The period of a Sea Island's history before connection to the mainland. For Hilton Head Island that period ended May 1956 when Hilton Head Island was connected to the mainland by a drawbridge; the lifestyle of Islanders before the bridge; Ex: A Before the Bridge House. See After the Bridge. Native Americans were the first inhabitants of Hilton Head and most other Sea Islands. The Spanish briefly inhabited Hilton Head, Saint Helena and other Beaufort area Sea Islands in the 1500's leaving "Spanish Wells," on Hilton Head now a neighborhood where they dug fresh water wells. Then in 1663 came William Hilton the Englishman for whom Hilton Head is named. The French also briefly occupied Beaufort area Sea Islands. Between the late 1860's and the late 1960's Hilton Head Island's population of between 2000 and 3000 was entirely Gullah (west African descendants) with the exception of a few Whites (European descendants). However White Northern business families owned about two thirds of the Island's 30,000 acres which they sold to resort developers in the early 1950's for less than $100 per acre.(see also after the bridge)
Benne	Sesame seeds (a member of the sesame family) – candy made from benne; the plant that produces benne grown by native islanders before development.
Big gun Shoot (at "Bay Pint")	The arrival of approximately (according to some historians) 12,000 Union troops at Hilton Head in November 1861 and the subsequent shelling of confederate forces on Bay Point, an Island on the other side of the Port Royal Sound, as described later by the jubilant Africans who until then had been enslaved.

B	Definition
Binya	Native of the island. One who has a long island ancestry; an elder lifelong resident of the island.
Bogging	A walk through the mud in the back creeks of islands on low tide, capturing crabs with a forked stick. Before the advent of commercial crab traps, crabs were so abundant that one could bog through the mud with a sack using a pronged stick to pick up dozens of crabs within an hour. Thus 'going bogging this afternoon' was a common vernacular. Anecdote: Bunny Jarvin(not his real name), a rather hefty middle aged man was bogging for a meal of crabs when he encountered soft mud, unexpectedly sinking to his waste. After trying in vain to lift himself leg-by-leg and sinking deeper, he began hollering loudly for help. Nearby neighbors heeding his call hurried toward the creek. Upon seeing them, Mr. Jarvin, noticing the flood tide was now above his waste, began to panic and thought his neighbors were moving too slowly. So he loudly expressed his feeling in classic Gullah: Oonuh come on if oonah da come, if oonuh na comin oonuh tun roun an go bak home. Of course his understanding, caring neighbors ignored Mr. Jarvin's thankless expression and assisted him out of the mud. Bunny Jarvis is therefore the bogging legend of all times.
Boneless ham	A watermelon; used humorously because of the regularity of watermelon in traditional Gullah family meals and snacks.
Booga hag	a person with unusual facial features, ugly; one who frightens as a Booga hag.
Boogie man	An unattractive man, ugly in appearance; a fictitious character that produces fear.

B	Definition
Brier Patch	A small area of plants with spurs; the proverbial place of happiness as depicted in the Gullah folktale of The Fox and the Rabbit. Rabbit tricked Fox by pretending that Bro' Fox could do anything except throw him in the brier patch. In fact that's where he feels very much at home. Thus, the legend: "he put me in the brier patch"(I liked what happened to me even though he thought he did harm to me.)
Broad Creek	The narrow body of water that nearly divides Hilton Head Island from its Southern end past its mid-section (Matthews Drive). Traditionally Broad Creek harbored abundant shrimp, fishes, oysters, and crab. Considered one of Hilton Head Island's "feeding troves," it was also the main water route used in traveling from the Island to Savannah. Since advent of modern resort development non point source pollutants have affected oysters in Broad Creek. Used primarily for recreational boat traffic, there is an on-going challenge to keep Broad Creek free from pollution.
Broom grass	A tall, slender jointed plant that grows wild in undeveloped areas of most sea islands; a broom when tied together in a bunch, to sweep the yard or house; Young girls also made dolls from broom grass using its roots as the head and hair.
Buckra	A white man, master, boss man.
Burial Society	A traditional organization established to provide care for members when they become sick and financial benefit to a named benefactor upon a member's death. Burial societies were active throughout the islands before modern development. On Hilton Head Island, Workers of Charity, Rose of Sharon, Farmers Club, Lily of the Valley, were typical names.

C	Definition
Cast Net	A net made of cotton yarn traditionally woven specifically for catching either fish or shrimp from the local creeks and rivers. A nets that is made for catching both fish and shrimp is called a poor man's net since the person cannot afford a net made specifically for either.
Casting	The act of flinging a fish or shrimp net (usually from a bateau) for the purpose of catching fish or shrimp. "Going casting" implies one is going to the creek to attempt at catching fish or shrimp.
Chinquapin	A member of the chestnut tree family that bears similar nuts. These trees grew abundantly in the Sea Islands before modern resort development. Children made decorative beads with the nuts for wearing to school from which they ate heartily during recess.
Christmas	A table spread of delicious indigenous foods and drinks– meats, fruits, vegetables, berry wines, ciders, etc. served to friends and neighbors during the Christmas holiday season. Come have some ... at my house. Island natives traditionally make house-to-house visits during the Christmas holiday to share Christmas; December 25th the holiday celebrating the birth of Christ.
Christmas Club	An organization of adult neighbors for the purpose of saving cash to make essential purchases for Christmas. Monthly meetings are held at neighbors' houses on a rotating basis from January until early December when savings plus proceeds from fund-raisers are distributed. Before commercial banks, the treasurer was responsible for keeping all revenues in a 'safe' place at home.
Coffee	The nickname for a dark skinned Black person, highly contemptuous before the "Black and proud" era of the 1960's.

C	Definition
Comya	One who comes from another place and takes up residence on the island. An immigrant to the island; One whose ancestry is not of the island; one who came after the bridge.
Coota	A small turtle, the terrapin or tortoise found in fresh water ponds around the island. Coota soup with rice is a traditional island cuisine.
Crabbing	The procedure used in gathering crabs for a meal or commercial. A piece of cotton yarn used in net weaving about 10 feet (or longer if using a pier or boat) with a pound to 2 pound weight (scrap iron) and a piece of fish is attached and emerged in the tidal creek from the shore. A "dip net" made with chicken fence wire attached to a circular piece of 1/8 thick inch wire nailed to a three-foot handle used for scooping the crab as it feeds on the bait. This same basic method was used in traditional commercial crabbing which required a line of several hundred feet along creek and river shores with bait (ham skin or bull nose) at one to two feet intervals. The crabber in a bateau with barrels rows along the line dipping crabs from the bait and depositing them into the barrels.
Crick	Creek; A relatively narrow body of water within the interior or back of islands. As Broad, Old House, and Skull Creeks on Hilton Head Island.
Cuffe	A black person. (Origin unknown to this author). Perhaps used in honor of Paul Cuffee an outstanding promoter of freedom for Black people during slavery.
Cuz	A cousin, a relative. A term used in expressing kinship.

D	Definition
Dä	in the act of, are Ex. You da do (are doing); da walk (walking) Sometimes used to show third person. Ex. Him da man. (He is the man.) To pick out. Ex. da da Joe. (That is Joe.)
Da (day)	here or there. Ex. He da Spanish Wells. (He is at Spanish Wells.) He da da. (He is there). I da ya. (I am here).
Daufuskie Day	Founded in December 1976, it is a celebration of Gullah folkways, food ways, and other cultural features. Devil crab is a delicacy usually served and other unique Gullah cultural features of Daufuskie Island. The celebration is usually held in June.
Decoration Day	Memorial Day; formerly so called because the graves of soldiers were honorably decorated with flags and flowers; a very special festive holiday in the Sea Islands (the city of Beaufort, S.C.) among only Gullah people between the end of the American Civil war and the 1970's when whites joined in observing the holiday.
Deef	deaf
Deer tongue	Another regional term for Musk; a clustered leaf fragrant plant that grows close to the ground in island forests. Deer tongue was harvested by adults and children daily during the summer and sold to local merchants. The plant is dried in the yard on blankets, and then sold by the weight. It takes many, many plants after drying to make up a pound. The buyers of Deer tongue paid about 5 cents per pound. The weekly earnings of a harvester were about $7.00.

D	Definition
Deke	Deacon; used affectionately in greeting and referring to a community member who has earned the status of Deacon in the church.
Det message	Death message. The message telling of a community member's death, usually brought by a person on a Marsh Tacky (horse) rapidly riding through the community while loudly shouting out the message that the person had just passed away—"Monday dead"(Monday has died) Ex. John bi bring da det message. (John brought the death message).
Digout	A small rowboat used in creeks around the islands for gathering seafood such as oysters, shrimp and crab. Although descriptive of the hued log models of Native Americans by which some were made, most of these canoe-like boats used by Gullahs were framed with single boards.

E	Definition
Edgar Hurst	A large passenger ferryboat owned and operated by businessman Charlie Simmons during the 1930's and 1940's. It was the first private-owned gas engine-powered boat available to Hilton Head Islanders for transportation between Hilton Head and Savannah. Before the advent of the Edgar Hurst in 1928 Islanders traveled to Savannah via sailboat, most of them made by their owners, and taking as long as three days to reach port. The Edgar Hurst made two trips weekly to Savannah.It left Hilton Head early Tuesday and Friday mornings from Harrison Landing (now Simmons' Fishing Camp) making a stop for Daufuskie passengers and freight arriving at Savannah early afternoon returning to Hilton Head the following afternoon. The boat transported passengers with their freight: watermelon, butter beans, fish, crabs, chicken, turkeys berries for sales at the market in Savannah.

E	DEFINITION
Emancipation Proclamation	A document issued by President Abraham Lincoln in September 1862 and officially read and effected January 1, 1863 freeing all enslaved people of states in rebellion against the Union. The reading of the document at Camp Saxon at Port Royal, South Carolina where hundreds of enslaved Africans gathered, is widely known as the first reading.
Enty	Isn't that so, are you? Isn't that right?

F	DEFINITION
Fa	to, for
Fa good	Permanent; for a long time. Ex: He came home fa good. (He came home to stay).
Fish net	A handmade net for catching fish as distinguished from a shrimp net. See cast net
Fishing	The act of catching fish.
Fix	To inflict evil spirit on a person usually on behalf of a third person for the purpose of doing physical harm through witchcraft. See Voodoo, Root man.
Fo day	Before day; before dawn; anytime between about 1 a.m. and day break. "Fo day in the morning."
Fo de bridge	See before the bridge. The period before the first bridge connecting Hilton Head Island to the mainland in 1956.
Fort Howell	Located on Beach City Road on Hilton Head Island. Now a preserved historic site, this unfinished fort was begun by Colored Troops in 1864 to protect Mitchellville, one of the first free settlements in the South. Both projects were abandoned when the U.S. Government ceased all Civil War reconstruction activities.

F	Definition
Freedmen	Persons (African men and women) who were released from enslavement by the Emancipation Proclamation in 1863. Later those and other African men and women were officially freed by the Thirteenth Amendment to the U.S. Constitution. A large number of Freedmen occupied the Sea Islands between 1863 and 1865, many of whom came from the mainland seeking refuge among the Union forces that occupied in the Sea Islands.
Funeral sermon	Eulogy—traditionally delivered six months after burial of the deceased lessening the burden of sorrow on the family. This practice was also due to time and transportation constraints (before the bridge) of the preacher almost all of whom resided on the mainland

G	Definition
Geechee	A gullah person. Descendant of the African rice coast. A person of African descent native to the Georgia and South Carolina Coast. A black person who likes rice and/or speaks the Gullah language. See Gullah.
Ghost	The spirit of a deceased person. The haunting image of the deceased; ghosts are often seen where murders occurred and near graveyards. Persons who are born with a veil over their face have special ability to see ghosts. Profanity, sulfur and hags are believed to negate ghosts.
Going down	Giving birth to a child. The time at which birth is given. (The size of the mother's stomach is reduced) Ex: When are you going down? Bertha gone down.

G	Definition
Graveyard	A cemetery. A burial ground created, with few exceptions, near a natural body of water, either a creek or a river, or in undisturbed forests. This practice is perpetuated due to the belief that the spirit of the deceased travels across water back to Africa. These sites are often in conflict with plans of resort developers who sometimes violate Gullah customs and state law by disturbing them. Graveyards are sacred grounds where one should not trek unnecessarily. Traditional Gullah graves are often decorated with favorite items of the deceased.
Gullah	A descendent of the people of the ancient West African rice coast from where people were enslaved and imported to the United States and enslaved; Blacks who settled in the isolated Sea Islands of Georgia and South Carolina after the Emancipation Proclamation; the culture of Sea Island Blacks distinguished by a rice diet, close family ties, spirituality, folktales, lore, and beliefs. The language or dialect spoken by these people. Ex.Tun 'roun ya le' mi see who yo da. (Turn around so I can see who you are)
Gullah Celebration	Began in 1997. A celebration of Gullah Cultural features, (i.e., food ways, folklores, art forms) this celebration takes place during the entire month of February on Hilton Head Island.
Gullah Festival	A fundraising celebration of Gullah Cultural features, (i.e., food ways, folklores, art forms). This celebration usually takes place Memorial Day weekend in Beaufort.

G	Definition
Gumbo	Okra; A delicious soup prepared with a mixture of okra, and other ingredients including chicken, crab, shrimp, green and lima beans. Also, any mixed soup of vegetables and meats even without okra and usually highly seasoned with a variety of herbs.

H	Definition
Hag	An elder woman, usually the eldest female community member. The spirit of Hags is believed to attempt smothering certain people while they sleep at night.
Half on it	A children's game by which a hand shake agreement between two persons gives each the right to half of the other's content in hand by a simple call of "half on it" unless the defense call of "no half" is made before the offender calls.
Hand	Good luck acquired from a voodoo person, usually for a fee, for gaining wealth or for bettering one's condition. Ex. As soon as I get paid I'm going and get a hand.
Heirs property	Undivided, ancestral land traditionally occupied by some descendants, while others live elsewhere usually in Northern cities. Modern resort development of coastal land often results in partition sales of ancestral land when developers or speculators purchase the interest of one or more heirs, who live elsewhere. This practice has resulted in the loss of a tremendous amount of land among Gullah people.
Hide and seek	A popular traditional recreation game in most neighborhoods. The object of which is to have a member of the group hide while the others are not watching except one member who announces when to begin seeking the member who has hidden.

H	Definition
Hilton Head Island Native Community Association	An organized group established to improve economic and social conditions of Native Islanders and to preserve their assets. Other islands are establishing similar organizations to preserve Gullah Cultural Assets.
Hook N Line	A length (about 100 feet) of yarn (traditionally cotton) with two fish hooks and pieces of scrap irons as sinkers wound around a stick used for catching fish from local creeks and rivers. Shrimp is used for bait. Hook 'n line fishing accounted for most fish caught for meals and sold during spring, summer and fall.
Hoppin John	Peas (usually field peas) and rice cooked together (casserole-like) particularly on New Year's Eve as it is believed to bring good luck for the year. Recipe: Hoppin John 1/2 of 1 lb bag dried field peas 3 c. uncooked rice 2 ham hocks 2 strips salt pork (diced) salt & pepper to taste 1/3 c. chopped scallions (optional) – Boil ham hocks and salt pork together in about 5 cups of water for approximately 45 minutes. – Drain water off. – Add 3 cups of water to meat bring to a boil, reduce heat – Add peas and scallions; continue to boil. Keep adding water until brown gravy appears and peas are tender. – Add uncooked rice and let simmer on low heat. – Stir with fork, cook with top on about 30 minutes or until liquid is absorbed and grains of rice are tender, but dry.

H	Definition
Hoppin John (cont'd)	(Other meats may be substituted for ham hocks and salt pork.) Serves 8 –10.
Horseback	The back of a horse. The traditional common means of transportation throughout the island. Either bare or covered with a crocus sack on which the rider sits. I came by horseback.
How oonah[1] da do?	"How are you all doing?" Greetings in Gullah. Good morning, Good afternoon. [1] Oona means you in West African languages; Lorenzo Turner, *Africanisms in the Gullah Dialect*.
Huckleberry	A blue berry that grew abundantly in the forests of Hilton Head and other Sea Islands during spring before advent of resort development. Children harvested huckleberry for shipping to mainland market places and for mothers to make cobblers.
Hymn lining	To line a hymn; the reading of hymn verses to a church or praise house congregation during devotional service. The congregation follows the reading with a cappella singing verse by verse to a tone set by an experienced note singer. It's widely believed among most people that this tradition is attributable to limited number of hymnals as well as literate persons.

I	Definition
Indigo	A plant that produces a blue dye upon extraction by boiling water. The second crop employed during the plantation system, marketing of the crop ended soon after the American revolution.

J	Definition
Jigger (chigger)	Fleas, jigger fleas; African term for fleas.
Juke	disorderly.
Juke box	A phonograph that plays records by insertion of a coin.(nickels, dimes, quarters in early use)
Juke Joint	a building, usually small, used for housing a juke box with space for serving drinks, snacks and dancing. Juke joints are traditionally located in the same yard with the owner's home
Just Law	The law of the church. Violation of another member's rights by a fellow member is reported to the appropriate church leader for review under covenants of the church or the Just law. The problem is resolved in accordance with the Just law. The church could punish the victim if he/she takes the matter to the unjust law before seeking redress at the Just law. See unjust law.
K	**Definition**
Kin	Related by birth or marriage; Gullah people are conscientious in knowing their relatives. Many can trace family roots back several generations making it easy for one to know one's 19th cousin.
L	**Definition**
Landing (Boat Landing	A particular point on the Marsh creeks used by neighborhood residents to access the creeks and rivers. Bateaux are anchored at landings to be available for use in daily food gathering.
Left Pocket	A children's game in which a hand shake agreement between two persons gives each the right to the contents of the other's left pocket by a simple call of "left pocket" unless the defense call of "no left pocket" is made before the offender's call.

L	DEFINITION
Li	little, tiny Ex: da li gal (that little girl).
Life Ever-lasting	A long slender plant that grows wild in fields used as an herb for making tea for relieving cold symptoms. The plant is placed in water and steeped during winter nights making a bitter tea and served to children and adults at bedtime.
Long eye	Excessive greed; Always wanting another person's possession or wanting to acquire far more than is adequate.
M	**DEFINITION**
Marsh Tacky	A small swift horse native to the island used for farming and transportation. Its main diet is marsh grass. Very durable, it can work for long periods without rest. Widely believed to be descendants of an Arabian species left by the Spaniards during their Sea Islands exploration in the 16th Century. The marsh tacky has become an endangered species on the islands.
Mash (Marsh) edge	Dead marsh grass washed ashore. Mash edge is harvested and used for fertilizing fields for farming.
'Matos	Tomatoes; Tomatoes became a major commercial crop in the Sea Islands in early 1950's. It was the last major crop grown on Hilton Head island before resort development. Gullah adults and children earned needed cash during the summers in the mid 20th Century planting and harvesting tomatoes for a North Carolina farmer. Pickers were paid ten cents per basket (half bushel), luggers (those who tote the baskets to the graders) were paid eight cents per pair of baskets. Many truckloads of tomatoes were shipped from large open fields in sections now known as Hilton Head Plantation, Jenkins Island and locations in Spanish Wells.

M	Definition
Mi	Mi self tink me bi see you fo now. (I think I have seen you before.)
Mi na know	I don't know.
Mi na bi no	I did not know.
Midwife	A person, usually a middle-age woman of the community-trained in assisting mothers with birthing at home. Traditionally midwives were trained by the State Health Department for delivering babies among remote rural and Sea Island residents. Midwives often walked considerable distances to their patients after being contacted by the husband, who usually went to them by horseback when their spouse was ready to Go Down. Having an abundance of hot water available, which was supplied with a hand pump, insured sanitation.
Mitchellville	A settlement of freedmen established in 1862, on the Northern end of Hilton Head Island near the Port Royal Sound. Named for General Omsby Mitchel, the settlement was the first such in the South that enabled former enslaved Africans to begin living as free humans after more than two centuries of enslavement.
Monkey	Heat stroke or heat exhaustion—"the monkey got you" when either condition exists. To have "monkied" due to excessive heat.
Moss	Spanish moss, a grayish airborne subtropical plant that grows symbiotically on trees. Moss seems to grow more abundantly on the live oak tree, a prevalent species in the Sea Islands from which it hangs making the likeness of the weeping willow. Moss was a staple for cows during the winter when grass is scarce. Thus the quip among Gullah children when greeted with "hey," "hey fa hoss, cow eat moss".

M	Definition
Mourner	One who is mourning due to sorrow. Also a participant at the Mourning's Bench. See Mourner's Bench and Mourning.
Mourner's bench	A bench placed in front of the leader's podium at the Praise House or in front of the pulpit at Church for those who have not confessed their belief in Christ or have confessed a sinful act. These participants meditate as an appointed spiritual leader or a pastor offers a prayer in their behalf.
Mourning	The act of expressing sadness or sorrow. Traditional mourning for loss of Gullah husband expressed by the widow fully dressing in the color black from head to feet (including stocking/socks and shoes) daily for six months to one year.
Muckle	Wax myrtle, as commonly termed by Gullahs. A shrubbery plant native to the Sea Island, popularly used as an ornament in resort landscaping.
Mullatto Rice	Rice cooked with tomato sauce resulting in a reddish color, also called red rice. Most recipes include sausage, onion, green peppers, and other seasonings.
Mus (Musk)	See deer tongue.

N	Definition
Na	Don't. Ex: Mi na know how fa cast. (I don't know how to cast a net.)

O	Definition
Oona	You, you all. Ex: We glad fa see oona. (We glad to see you.)

O	DEFINITION
One a catch	A game played usually in the backyard with three persons (pitcher, catcher, batter), a ball, a bat and one base. The object of the game is to hit the ball and get to the base a considerable distance (60 feet to 90 feet) away and return to home plate before the ball is received by one of the two players covering the plate. If the ball is received at the plate before the batter arrives or if the ball is caught on the fly, the batter is out. The next person that bats is the catcher, the pitcher becomes the catcher and the batter becomes the pitcher and so on in rotation.
One room school	A small building without partition walls to separate classes; in the Sea Islands one-room schools contained wooden tables and benches to suit children from primers to sixth graders. Some one-room schools were built under the Julian Rosenwald-Booker T. Washington program. Reading, writing and 'rithmetic were basic subjects taught as each class in rotation either stood before the teacher or remained at their seats. A potbellied stove was positioned in the center of the room in most schools to supply heat. Children chopped the firewood that was supplied by parents. (see also Rosenwald School.)

P	DEFINITION
Palmetto	Nickname of the state of South Carolina; a species of palm widely grown along the coast of South Carolina. According to historians, palmetto was used in building a fort that helped to defeat the British during the Revolutionary War.

P	Definition
Penn Center	Founded in April 1862 on Saint Helena Island during the American Civil War by Laura Towne and Ellen Murray; widely acknowledged as the first school in the south for formerly enslaved Africans. Charlotte Forten, a Black teacher, joined Towne and Murray in October of that year. After 91 years of formal education service, the school became Penn Center, a community development center. The 50-acre original school campus is a National Historic Landmark District of more than twenty historic structures, making an enchanting conference center and a museum exhibiting the history of Penn School and the Gullah culture. During the Civil Rights Movement in the 1960's, the center was one of two main training and strategy sites for Dr. Martin Luther King and Movement workers.
Penn Center Heritage Days	Held annually the 2nd weekend in November, a celebration of Penn Center's contribution to education and the Gullah culture. Highlights folklore, food ways, and cultural arts through lectures, seminars, and performances.
Penn club	An organized group of former students and friends of Penn school and Penn Center who give ongoing dedicated moral and financial support to the institution.
Pie Back	Referring to one with a weak back; one who pretends to be fragile like piecrust; one that bending easily injures. Thus, a pie back job or a pie back person; One who shuns ordinary work and carefully selects work that requires little exertion.
Pilau (Perlow)	A rice dish made with either shrimp, oysters, beans, and herbs, spices, etc.

P	Definition
Poly Po John	Common name among Gullah people for a tall plant with a sturdy wooden stock draped with pods and scanty thin leaves. Also called indigo because of their similarities. Indigo was one of the main crops grown on southern plantations during the slavery period.
Praise House	A small one-room building located in each neighborhood, on most Sea Islands in which prayer meeting was held three times weekly – Sunday, Tuesday and Thursday evening. A community member is assigned to ring a cowbell at an appointed time in early evening to alert other community members of service time. One to two dozen members gathered and sang hymns and spirituals, testified and returned home after about two hours. The praise house also served as the disciplinary place where members were placed on the back seat when found guilty of breaking Christian doctrine – i.e., stealing from a neighbor or other mistreatment of a fellow community member.
Prawn	Shrimp, traditional large shrimp harvested by "prawn boat."
Prawn boat	A shrimp boat, a large boat with attached nets used for fishing off the ocean shore in catching prawn.
Pray	A traditional ritual followed to become a member of the church: To meditate for a period of time during which nightly dreams are recalled and told to a spiritual leader for interpretation, a sacred place in the forest is visited three times daily- fo day, midday and evening in determining eligibility for Baptism and subsequently church membership. Children after reaching age 8-10 prayed during summer vacation from school

P	DEFINITION
Pray (cont'd)	most of whom spend the entire summer socially isolated except for assigned chores, until they had "gotten through" (become eligible). This tradition is linked directly to West African practices.

R	DEFINITION
Red	Often used as a nickname for an extremely dark (sarcasm) or fair skinned person.
Red Bug	An insect that is prevalent on bushes and Spanish moss during spring and summer that causes itching. One may become infested when direct contact is made with these plants.
Rev	Reverend; used affectionately in greeting or referring to a community member who has achieved the status of reverend.
Rolling cans	A number of empty cans that are linked together with wire in a train-like fashion. Traditionally made by children in the backyard when toy stores were non-existent in the Sea Islands.
Root	The root of plants used for medicinal or witchcraft purposes. The root of plants or trees is sometimes used in preparation of the witchcraft.
Root man or Root Doctor	A person who practices witchcraft, sometimes using roots. One who prepares herbal medicine with plants or roots.
Rosenwald School	A one room schoolhouse in rural south built with funds generated by seed grant from philanthropist Julian Rosenwald and the advocating of Booker T. Washington. Distinguished by windows on only the south side of the building, several of these style schools were built in the Sea Islands in the 1920's and 1930's.

S	Definition
Salt Marsh	The marsh grass that grows in the saltwater creeks and rivers that surround most Sea Islands and coasts of South Carolina.
Saltwater	Surface water of creeks, rivers and oceans that surrounds most Sea Islands of S.C. Also, other east coast waterways may be salty.
Saltwater Geechee	One of the traditional colloquial terms for descendants of Africans who reside near saltwater rivers on the Sea Islands of South Carolina.
Scull	The skillful use of one oar at the stern of a bateau to push water away forcing it forward. Gullah people are very skillful at sculling because one pair of oars was often shared with another person. The act of sculling.
Sea Islands Festival	Usually held in September, a celebration of the Gullah culture in the Sea Islands around Charleston County, South Carolina. (Johns, James, Wardmalow, Edisto) featuring Gullah food, stories, art forms, etc.
Secede	To break away as South Carolina, the first state to do so did in 1861 from the U. S., which began the Civil War that eventually produced the 13th amendment to the U. S. constitution in 1865 freeing enslaved persons.
Seek	To pray. (See pray)
Settin up	a wake where neighbors sit with family of the deceased all night; the time when neighbors or burial society members sit with a bedridden sick member providing nursing care throughout the night.
Shake and Drop	A specific Gullah family recipe of hominy grits and bacon.

S	Definition
Shout	A sacred, religious dance in the Gullah culture, which is distinguished by careful movement of the feet avoiding the crossing of step, which would imply secular dancing. Shouting at social functions displays steps crossing and pronounced body movement. The rhythm for shouts is usually supplied by hand clapping, foot stomping or tapping a stick on the floor.
Skeeta	Mosquito, a skinny person, also skeet.
Skeeta halk	A dragonfly.
Soul	A person who has completed the seeking process to become a member of the church and is therefore a candidate for baptism; one who is seeking to become or is already a member of the church.
Spirit	See ghost.
Stand up stick	A fictitious stick that one (usually young boy or girl) is sent to retrieve from a neighbor, who in turn sends the person to another neighbor to whom he supposedly loaned the stick, who in turns sends the person to another until all neighbors have been contacted. Children who sit or stand idle in the company of adults are usually sent for the stand up stick if there are no chores to be done.
Still wake	A gathering of friends, neighbors and relatives at the praise house or home of the deceased. They sit in silence throughout the night thus a still wake. Food and beverages are served.
Sugar tip	Small ball of lard sprinkled with sugar wrapped in a cloth for the newborn used between breast feedings.
Sweet grass	A thin, scraggly grass that grows near the ocean and is used for making Gullah (sweet -grass) baskets.

S	Definition
Sweet grass bucket	See sweet grass; A coiled basket made of sweet grass traditionally used as a house utility. Now used chiefly as a commemorative art form.
Swimp (shrimp)	Shrimp, one of the popular shellfish harvested from local waters.
Swimp net	A cast net traditionally made with mesh sized appropriately for catching shrimp.

T	Definition
Taking up	The review for candidates' dreams by a committee of church leaders to verify their eligibility for baptism. See pray.
Tata	Sweet potato. Yam; Tata is a traditional crop of Gullah families. Roast' tata is done by placing potato under hot ashes in fireplace or outdoor fire.
Tatapoon	A delicious traditional dessert made of finely grated sweet potato, sugar, butter, lemon rind, and cinnamon, usually served during Christmas.
Tief	To steal, one who steals. Ex: e da tief. (He/she is a thief). (He/she is stealing).
Tote	To carry; Traditionally Gullah women carry (tote) items on their head.
Travel	The series of dreams experienced during the period of seeking to become a church member. A person is considered traveling as he or she moves from a status of ungodliness (before church membership) to a status of godliness (church membership).

U	Definition
Unjust law	The law of the government courts. Community members are restricted from participating in government court before reporting an offense to church leaders for review and an opportunity to mediate.
V	**Definition**
Vernon, the	The name of a passenger boat that transported people between Jenkins Island public dock on Hilton Head Island and Buckingham public dock on the mainland before the bridge. Operated by island businessmen Arthur Frazier. See Before the Bridge.
Voodoo	A practice of witchcraft in which practitioner usually administers good or evil spirit.
W	**Definition**
Wake	The gathering of family and friends at the home or church where body of the deceased lay the evening before the funeral. Wakes are very festive with those present telling stories about the deceased while traditional food and drinks are served. See also Still Wake.
Walking cans	A pair of large cans emptied of their contents with heavy stirrup-like strings attached through holes on opposite edge of one end on which a person stands holding the strings for balance while walking.
Watch night	The gathering of community members at the praise house or church or at someone's house from about 9 o'clock until midnight on New Year's Eve. During the gathering, members sing traditional spirituals, give testimonies of the past year and express wishes for the coming year until time to watch for the New Year's arrival. A person (watchman) is sent outside about 15 minutes before the midnight to watch for the New Year. Before watches were available, the

W	Definition
Watch night (cont'd)	"Watchman" watched the moon to determine when midnight arrived. Everyone kneels at their seat while the leader calls out to the watchman for the times left in the old year as he leads the gathering in prayer. The sequence continues until the watchman announces arrival of the New Year, which evokes shouting and jubilance.
Watchman	The appointed person who watches for the New Year's arrival at watch night services. See Watch Night.
We glad fa see oonah	We are glad to see ya'll.
Wharf	A dock used by community for fishing. Even though most wharfs were private, community members were free to use any Hilton Head wharf before the bridge.

Y	Definition
Ya	Here
Yeah	Yes
Yeddy	To hear
Ye Yent	Is that True!
Yez	Ears

Gullah Proverbs

1. dog got four feet but can't walk but one road

Translation: No matter how many things you'd like to do, you can only do one thing at a time.

2. e teet da dig e grave

Translation: His/her teeth are digging his/her grave (he/she is overeating)

3. fox da watch de henhouse

Translation: The fox is protecting the henhouse. (a crook is in charge of protecting the items from crooks.)

4. milk ain't dry off e mout yet

Translation: The person is very young, too young for the assignment.

5. every sick ain't fa tell de doctor.

Translation: Do not tell your doctor every ailment (no matter how close the friend or relative do not confide everything in him/her.)

6. every frog praise e ownt pond.

Translation: Every frog praises his pond.(it is expected that one speaks favorable of one's self or one's kin folk disregarding the accuracy of the statement)

7. Cow need e tail more than fly time.

Translation: Cows need their tail for more reasons than brushing away flies.(always express gratefulness for the simplest personal favor because you may need a favor from the same person again for a different reason)

8. Servants ease your feet but ache your heart.

Translation :If you want to assure your satisfaction with a chore, do it yourself.

9. New broom sweeps clean but old broom gets the corners.

Translation: A new person may appear to have all the answers for challenges of the job, but the person who had been there knows better the intricacies of the job.

10. Lil' pitcher got big ears.

Translation: Be careful what you say around little children, they be able to understand more than you think they can.

GULLAH FOLKTALE

Gullah Version

Why Bro Cat na da wash e face fo e eat e brekwas

Once upon a tim fo day was clean, one monin Bro rat bina wonda roun de rim ob barril wuh bin half ful wid watuh an bin slip an fal een.

E binah tri fa git out, but ebry tim e fa grab de wal e slip and fal bac in da watuh. Wen e bin dun bout gib up e yeddy a nise.

Da nise binah bro cat who bina saach fa brekwas. Bro cat cock e yez and yeddy de watuh da splas. E clim up de side de barril and lok een and bi see bro rat. E sae how yu git down en da bro rat? Bro rat sae, maan a bina wak roun de edge ob de barril fa lok een an a slip an a Fall een. Eef you hep me fa git outa ya I leh you eat me fa brekwas. Bro cat say, fa true? Bro rat say yeah fa true.

Bro cat gon and clim up tuh de top ob de barril and bi

English Version

Why Bro Cat Does Not Wash His Face Before Breakfast.

Once upon a time, Bro Rat was wandering around the rim of a barrel half filled with water and slipped and fell in.

He was futilely trying to climb up the slippery side of the barrel when bro cat, looking for breakfast, heard Bro Rat splashing in the barrel. Bro Cat climbed up the side of the barrel to see who was in there and saw Bro Rat.

"How did you get yourself in such a fix?"asked Bro Cat.

Bro Rat answered, "man I was curious about what was inside the barrel and slipped and fell in. If you help me get out, I'll let you eat me."

"Would you really?" asked Bro Cat. "Sure I'll let you eat me," answered Bro Rat. "That's a deal," said Bro Cat. Then he reached down rech down and grab bro rat by e tail. E bi lay bro rat on de broad sid de barril and bi staat fa eat bro rat. Bro rat halluh; oh no bro cat yu haffa leh me dri fus fo you choke yourself tuh det. Go wush you face wile a dry,

Bro cat gon fa wush e face an wen e bi git bac e brekwas bin gon. Bro cat nebuh wush e face fo brekwas from dat dae tuh dis.

with his two front paws and grabbed Bro Rat by the tail and laid him on a nearby board.

As Bro Rat laid there soggy, Bro Cat approached to begin his meal. "Oh no!" screamed Bro Rat, you don't want to eat me like this. Man, my wet hair will choke you to death. You'd better let me dry so you can take my hair off. Why don't you go and wash your face while I dry here in this sun," Bro Rat advised.

Bro Cat went and washed his face, but when he returned Bro Rat had disappeared. From that day to this, Bro Cat never washed his face before he eats breakfast.

Traditional Gullah Neighborhoods

Most traditional Gullah neighborhoods in the Sea Islands are uniquely autonomous, similar to their ancestral villages in West Africa. Historically they contained clustered extended families; a Praise House; essential skills bearers; (cast net makers, boat builders, etc;) spiritual leaders; food processing mills (sugarcane and corn) and access to the waterway. Together these qualities ensured sustainability.

Yet their own particular produced goods, services, and natural environment brands each of these neighborhoods.

Like other Sea Islands, Hilton Head Island exemplifies this phenomenon in its ten villages that were established in the late 1860's:

Stoney - the gateway to Hilton Head; this neighborhood was once "downtown Hilton Head." The post office, juke joints and grocery stores owned by the Drayton and Simmons families were located here. The most recent active midwife who is memorialized by the street named Adrianna Lane lived in Stoney.

Jonesville – Known for its wheelwrighters and shoemakers, this neighborhood also had its businessmen and carpenters. Perhaps the main distinguishing characteristic is The Church of Christ ("Sanctified" church), where various musical instruments and rhythmic drumming substantiated connections to African spiritually.

Spanish Wells is the neighborhood extending from the river used by Spanish explorers who came up the waterway from Florida and dug fresh water wells there in the 1500s. Its residents are known for their extensive maritime activities in the Broad Creek – fishing, crabbing and oyster harvesting. Prominent businessman Charles Simmons, Sr. operated the Island's main variety store there for many years.

Simmons Fishing Camp –established about 1928 as Harrison Landing the site of the embarkation point of transportation to Savannah. Recently Charles Simmons' family, who were owners of the first Gullah owned passenger/freight boat and the Island's main variety store, rebuilt the original dock. After the bridge, a more modern building named Simmons Fishing Camp was built to accommodate visitors and fishermen.

Gardner –Marshland –this neighborhood is part of large acreage purchased by an African American immediately after the Civil War. Today an extended Gullah family occupies a portion of the land, however, most of the original purchase is now known as Indigo Run, a private gated community.

Chaplin - named for one of the Planters – families whose lifestyle focused on farming and fishing settled this community. These families were particularly skilled in netting large fishes from the beach – trout, drum, bass, etc. This neighborhood also hosted picnics sponsored by other neighborhoods that came to the beaches several times during the summer. Basket weaving and fishnet makers were distinguished residents. Today this neighborhood is being heavily encroached by a beach park and other mainstream resort establishments. Central Oak Grove Baptist Church, Driessens' grocery and Abe's restaurant have been the pillar of the Gullah heritage in Chaplin. Conglomerates now own

Singleton, Burke and Bradley, once Gullah family-owned Beaches that hosted many excursions of Black people to the island during racial segregation in the 50's and 60's.

Union Cemetery/Grassland, established during the Civil War for Union soldiers, this cemetery has been active ever since. After the soldiers' graves were transferred to the national cemetery in Beaufort, Union Cemetery was adopted by the adjacent neighborhood where several families settled and proceeded to establish successful farming enterprises. One of the most successful Gullah farm families is the Whites who produced tons of watermelons, sweet potatoes, beans – all African related crops, that in the early days were shipped to Savannah market place, in sail boats from the nearby shores. This family subsequently produced educators who served in Pennsylvania and New Jersey as well as locally. In recent years, a family member converted a portion of the land to establish a model affordable housing cluster for working people.

Mitchellville/Fish Haul (Bay Gaul) perhaps the first community established in the U.S. for free African Americans after the Emancipation Proclamation. Settled in 1862 with more than 1500 persons, this was the same general area where over 12,000 union troops had landed in November 1861. An essential part of the Port Royal Experiment for several years, the newly freed African lived in this village until the Reconstruction effort was abandoned. The population subsequently dispersed to other parts of the island. This is also the neighborhood where one of the two Civil War opposing Drayton brothers lived. The marker at Fish Haul verifies this fact. People in this area are known for their tradition in fishing for drum fish and big game hunting. The

Cherry Hill School House and the St. James Baptist Church are two structures that contrast the eras between 1863 when Gullahs controlled the island's social, education, and economic institutions and the present resort mainstream control.

Queen Chapel AME Church (Marker) is the site of one of the first AME Church organizations in South Carolina when – in 1865 – a group of African Americans landed on the beach at Mitchellville and organized a church under oak trees at this site.

First African Baptist Church – Organized in 1863 at Mitchellville – was the first Church for free African Americans on Hilton Head Island. The church was later moved to its present site.

Squire Pope – Gum Tree Road is perhaps the largest Gullah neighborhood in population and area on Hilton Head Island. Mt. Calvary Missionary Baptist Church has always been one of its defining institutions. Two model housing projects, by the Island's first Gullah developer Thomas C. Barnwell, demonstrate the changes in land use among Gullahs – Cedar Wells and Wild Horse Court occupy former watermelon and beans and cattle fields. Families of the neighborhood were once distinguished farmers and shrimp boat captains. The first organized community fishing cooperative was established there on Skull Creek in 1968. It has since been sold to a private businessperson.

A portion of Broad Creek on Hilton Head Island.

Sand dunes on Hilton Head Island beaches.

One room schoolhouse.

Juke Joints of yesteryears on Hilton Head Island.

Access to the former "colored" beach of the 1950's.

Abandoned pantry of yesteryear.

The Atlantic Ocean.

The Palmetto, native tree of South Carolina.

Tabby Ruin

Live Oak Tree.

Above: Union Cemetery
Left: Drayton Plantation Marker.

Mitchellville site historic marker.

TROLLEY AND OTHER MARSH TACKIES

I thought my grieving would never end after *Trolley*, our beloved Marsh Tackey died. Like all Marsh Tackies he had come from a long line of a mix breed horses. He had joined our family in the 1940's when I was a kid. *Trolley* was certainly not always ideally gentle and loveable, once pawing my older brother Herb leaving a huge contusion on his forehead, insistently biting at us in defiance of being bridled and darting off the trail to dismount his rider. But upon his death in the 1960's at twenty-something after a long illness from a festered shoulder, none of these incidents came to mind. My love of horses and my appreciation of *Trolley's* faithful service to our family dominated my sorrowful thoughts. He had spent most of his nearly twenty-five year life span plowing fields, pulling wagons, and serving as mount for family members in their travels to the store, to the Post Office, and to church and other places. And I remembered the excitement in his whinnies (loud sometimes shrilling sounds from horses) during springtime whenever he saw a young mare, his forward pointed ears when he was pleased or carefully listening, and his batted ears when he was displeased about something. And throughout his life Trolley had dutifully responded to the regular command of "giddap" but was always grateful for the intermittent "whoa" command that would now be eternal.

Depending on the source, the ancestry of *Trolley* and other Marsh Tackies may include the Arabian horse, the Shetland pony as well as larger breed of horses. *Trolley* had come from a then more recent interbreeding of Marsh Tackies on Hilton Head Island. Like most of his Sea

Islands colleagues he was only about fifteen *hands* (the unit measurement for horse heights) and thrived on small portions of grain, salt marsh, land grass, and fresh water. Handsome with a reddish brown coat and a white streak extending from between his big brown eyes down to his gaping nostrils, Trolley was a tough, sure-footed horse. He was born to a Marsh Tackey named *Pink* who belonged to my Uncle Johnny and Aunt Tilda of the Grassland neighborhood. Amicable negotiations between my father and Uncle Johnny brought Trolley to our Spanish Wells neighborhood. Customarily families named their Marsh Tackies for one of the original owner's family members, but our family fittingly chose to name ours *Trolley*, since much of his duties would be transporting people and goods.

When the Sea Islands were mainly agrarian, and before automobiles became as affordable as they are today, nearly every Gullah family had at least one Marsh Tackey. Two Marsh Tackies in a family was commonplace. And they came in various beautiful colors: sleek black and white, brown, gray, grayish brown and other hues. When I was growing up on Hilton Head Island in the 1940's and 1950's there were nearly fifty Marsh Tackies in my neighborhood of Spanish Wells alone. Marsh Tackies represented great hope for productive crops, family mobility, the transfer of goods, and message transmission. And neighbors would share each other's Marsh Tackey whenever circumstances required certain qualities such as swiftness, strength or sensibility. An indelible presence on the landscape in the Sea Islands, Marsh Tackies boosted the capacity of families to grow and gather food; to gather firewood for cooking and heating; to quickly transmit essential messages; and to transport people and goods. They are remembered in their neighborhoods for one or more characteristics such as sensibility, swift or slow afoot, strength, obedience, kindness, meanness, stubbornness, beauty, courage and endurance. Fathers mounted them to fetch the midwife at birthing times and hitched them to wagons for hauling remains of deceased loved ones to the graveyard.

Kieti, A family Marsh Tackey and another Marsh Tackey graze on Native Islander's pasture.

Earlier Marsh Tackies in Our Family

I can barely remember Sworee, our extended family's old sleek black stallion and *Maggie* an old brown mare, named for my mother's sister, who preceded Trolley in death. However, I can vision *Sworee's* long black body with what seemed to be a disproportionate long coarse tail. My paternal grandparents originally owned him. Those who remember *Sworee* immortalize him for his clumsiness and slowness afoot. Although he fulfilled his duty whenever requested, most everyone shunned *Sworee* in favor of another available neighborhood Marsh Tackey if the chore required quickness. Likewise I remember Maggie's bony brown body moving slowly down the road as a mount. My maternal grandparents owned her. She too was used sparingly when chores required quickness. They were both used by my extended family to carry out horse duties and they were both eventually relieved of certain duties that required quickness and heavy lifting after *Trolley* arrived.

Trolley's Introduction to Work and Neighbors

Although *Trolley* was young, strong and highly energetic, he had to be trained (horse broken) to perform the usual farm related and other duties like other young Marsh Tackies, several of whom had become distinguished for their particular prowess. And *Trolley* was not unusual among young powerful unbroken horses in posing a threat to health and safety of anyone who would try to engage him in work activity. That is why some people would have their young stallion Marsh Tackies castrated reducing the Tackies' power so they could better mange them. Early on my father had *Trolley* castrated assuring himself that we children could manage the young strong creature while he was away at work down river in Savannah. Then he assigned my teenage brother George and first cousin Clarence to break *Trolley* into the world of horse work. I remember seeing them harnessing *Trolley* and hitching the trace chains-singletree unit to objects, alternating the sizes and weights as *Trolly* learned how to use his muscles efficiently. After some days of this enterprise George and Clarence valiantly faced the perils and gave *Trolley* his first experience at being a mount for energetic young boys. Soon *Trolley* was sufficiently disciplined to join the work force with other renowned veteran Marsh Tackies in our neighborhood.

There was *Paul,* a relatively large thick legged, stallion who was always prancing with abundant energy unused from limited field work. Living almost next door to my cousins where *Paul* resided, I observed that *Paul* was used mostly as a mount for various errands. We could hear his heavy gallop a quarter mile away as my playmate cousin Elmer would jockey him to pick up items from a store at Jonesville, the adjacent neighborhood nearly two miles away, or deliver fish from his fisherman father to local neighbors. I do not recall ever seeing *Paul* pull a plow or wagon, but he was an excellent mount.

Further down the road from where we lived was *Big George* a castrated stallion, perhaps the largest horse owned by any Gullah family on Hilton Head Island. *Big George* was a model workhorse of legendary strength that one of our neighborhood sons had bought for his mother with earnings from his World War II military duty.[1] Standing at about twenty or more *hands* with a slick dark brown coat, *Big George* was indeed a quarter horse who our neighborhood relied on to perform duties that were beyond the capacity of Marsh Tackies. And he was often the center of attraction when there was a need to employ his awesome strength in moving heavy loads or busting tough farm grounds with a simple single tree-hitched plow. *Big George* also was considered a playmate to the neighborhood children, as he would swim with them as they recreated at the boat landing. The entire Spanish Wells neighborhood mourned intensely when *Big George* died accidentally from an impaled fence pole one hot summer day.

---

[1] By the end of the Korean War in 1953, a public ferry operated between the Island and the mainland thus inspiring military service persons to buy cars instead of horses with their earnings.

Pride of Marsh Tackey Ownership

There was a certain level of pride that Mash Tackey ownership brought to families that might be amusing to many in today's modern Sea Islands. In our family one tale centered on *Sworee* whose work performance was mentioned earlier, and *Maggie* my maternal grandfather's nag, retiring from fieldwork and becoming regular mounts for my Sister Regina and cousin Cassie and others for errands. Like today when the model make, and condition of one's automobile is considered a statement of one's social status so did the appearance and health of one's Marsh Tackey influence one's relationship with other youth in the 1940's and 1950's. But to keep *Sworee* and *Maggie* attractive was becoming a futile effort. Despite increased portions of feed and an unusual amount of time and energy spent grooming their coats, *Sworee* and *Maggie* had reached an age that no make over procedures of the time could disguise. While their appearance did not deter Regina and Cassie from using them for mounts, my brother George would evoke laughter from family members when he would walk the two miles to the Post Office rather than mount one of the nags and encounter teasing from his schoolmates.

Other legends include the time when a man brought the end of his Marsh Tackey's range rope inside the house through a bedroom window and tied it too his bed after he had been victimized by horse rustling. The rustler simply untied the end from the horse's neck and made off with the horse to run his errand.

Then there was the young man who regularly mounted his Marsh Tackey to visit the young lady that he was courting in another neighborhood several miles away. One of his peers who was competing for the young lady's loyalty would repeatedly unfasten the waiting Marsh

Tackey while the young man visited, leaving him without a mount on which to return home. The courtship eventually ended after the young man became tired of having to walk the several miles back home.

A Work Horse Indeed

In time *Trolley* became the family's main workhorse with all the usual duties: plowing, firewood hauling, and a mount for local travels. He performed these duties primarily for our household, but was often loaned out to our extended family for the same duties until they acquired their own Marsh Tackies. Perhaps his busiest season was the Spring. On a typical day beginning **fo day** clean he would be required to plow fields for or planting corn, peas, squash sweet potatoes, sugar cane, low bush butter beans, watermelon, etc; until noon then pull a wagon through the forest until it was filled with firewood and haul it two to three miles to a house in the neighborhood. Then after a brief afternoon rest and a meal of sweet feed -- corn mix or a bundle of freshly cut green salt marsh he would be mounted for a three mile hike through the sandy trail to church. There he would feed on sprouting grass until church service was over and deliver his mount back home about ten o'clock at night.

No doubt the most leisurely season for *Trolley* was Winter when except for wood hauling that required him to pull a wagon through rugged terrain, he was allowed to run loose in the fields and forest with other Marsh Tackeys. Whenever we needed to coral him we would interrupt his frolicking with our usual *coub- coub* call showing him an ear of corn to which he would respond by eagerly trotting to the caller.

Trolley was certainly a standout personality. Overall he was as good as any Marsh Tackey his age and size Island wide. While fieldwork was his main purpose he also liked to compete in running with other Marsh Tackies whenever the opportunity presented itself on errands. Although he never competed in the annual Christmas Marsh Tackey Race on Marshland Road, he never lost a casual sprint to any mounted Marsh Tackey challenger.

But not all stories about *Trolley* are pleasant ones. There was the time in his early life when he deliberately pawed a huge knot my on brother Herb's forehead as he served him a bucket of water. Where upon my father evoked hilarity among us when he promptly tied *Trolley* to the pecan tree and applied a few heavy whip lashes while commanding that Trolley stop " kicking the boy." Even though he ceased pawing, biting became his usual behavior whenever he was irritable.

Later in life *Trolley* evoked serious concerns from family and neighbors when we found him lying near death in the sweet potato field early one fall morning. During the night he had broken loose from his stake and overeaten on potato vines. Unable to chew the vines finely enough for digestion, he had developed a severe case of colic. My father hurriedly followed the usual Gullah tradition in desperate situations and summoned neighborly help. Several able bodied men diligently responded and through much struggle managed to get *Trolley* to our backyard. Under our pecan tree our next-door neighbor, Mr. Mose, a heavily mustached Gullah who was experienced in horse remedies, directed the course of treatment. First with strategically placed ropes from limbs on the tree to *Trolleys* body they raised *Trolley* on shaky legs to his feet. Then employing a simply made wooden bit bridle, they widened *Trolley's* mouth allowing Mr. Mose to slowly pour a concoction of heated cooking oil and some other ingredients from a long narrow neck quart bottle down *Trolley's* throat. Almost instantly, to cheers from everyone, missiles of potato vines projected from *Trolley's* bowels and he was again as well as ever.

Emory S. Campbell on Marsh Tackey Cassie Mae in his backyard on Hilton Head Island in 1967.

Welcome Help and Uncertain Posterity

By and by to the family's delight three other wonderful Marsh Tackies in our extended family joined Trolley. Maggie's offspring Lucky, so named because he was the only one of hers that survived, never succeeded as a workhorse. As the workload increased, our family searched other sources to get help for Trolley. Uncle Pheris bought *Alice,* a beautiful gray mare from the Driessens in

Stoney, our grandparents bought *Hannah*, a reddish brown mare from the Barnwells in Squire Pope (both named for their respective sellers' wives) and later *Alice*'s filly who Uncle Sol acquired and named *Cassie Mae* in honor of his daughter. *Cassie Mae* would later give birth to a filly that I acquired and fittingly named Kieti, the Swahilli word for stubborn. Some fifteen years later the change in lifestyle at the Campbell family compound due largely to resort development moved me to sell *Kieti* to the Barnwells in Squire Pope. At this writing *Kieti*, at the approximate age of 36 is one of only two or three Marsh Tackies that still exist on Hilton Head Island.

"How Coastal Changes Have Influenced Gullah Spirituality"

I have chosen to inscribe this effort, Gullah Spirituality, as if I know enough about it. I will be the first to admit that perhaps I do not. My personal depth of experience in traditional Gullah spirituality is almost completely observational. All I know is that Gullah Spirituality seems to have changed during my lifetime. And perhaps it is due to the changes that have taken place in our coastal environment, the primary location of Gullah culture for centuries.

Therefore I hope you understand why I am a bit nervous about discussing anything about Gullah Spirituality except to point out some changes in the practice since the advent of resort development on the coast. My main focus, geographically, is the Hilton Head – St. Helena area although one might find these same changes everywhere along the coast between southern North Carolina and northern Florida.

Ever since accepting Christianity nearly two hundred years ago as their main spiritual base, Gullah People have relied on church service for their spiritual sustenance. This reliance, belief and confidence in the Christian Church came after considerable struggle to reconcile African spiritual traditions with Christianity.

In her superb study of Gullah religion in her book "A Peculiar People", Margaret Creel, discusses how Gullah people have blended their African beliefs with Christianity. She states: "Belief in ancestral spirits, in life after death, and in the significance of that future life gave funeral and burial rites a central place in African existence."

She goes on to state that "African reverence for departed members of the family and group remained a factor in Gullah religious life even after they accepted Christianity." For centuries Gullah people have exhibited substantial African spiritual belief in their practice of Christianity. But today in the Sea Islands we are observing that much of the fore-mentioned pronounced duality of Christian and African spirituality is strikingly subsiding. For example, at funerals Gullah people traditionally pass the youngest close relative of the deceased across the open grave. This practice according to Gullah belief repels the spirit of the deceased from returning for the child. But morticians, who fear that the family could hold them liable if the child is accidentally dropped in the grave, are discouraging that practice.

Today on Hilton Head Island Gullah Spirituality is practiced and essentially directed through six Christian based churches. Four are Baptists, one is African Methodist Episcopal, and one is Holiness/Sanctified. These churches range in membership numbers from 100 to as many as 300 native Islanders. Their edifices have changed since the advent of resort development from shapely frame white painted clapboards with wooden floors to masonry type buildings with cushion-like floor rugs that silence the foot stomping of prior days.

The oldest organized congregation among them is the First African Baptist Church that began in 1863 from which the other churches – Mt. Calvary, Central Oak Grove, St. James, and The Church of Christ – split during the last century and a half.

Currently with the exception perhaps of the Church of Christ, these churches function more like mainstream black churches than like the usual Gullah worship of early twentieth century years ago. Each of the churches conduct services every Sunday, a departure from the traditional rotating schedule of monthly communion service at a different church. These days each conducts its own monthly communion service. Music (choir with piano, organ, drums) dominates the service. The choir is expected to inspire the Pastor whose sermon is expected to inspire one's soul for 30 to 60 minutes and beyond the edifice until the next Sunday.

One is accepted for membership after confessing to the Pastor and members one's belief in Christ and after baptism in a pool of water of comfortable temperature located within the church sanctuary. In past years *Souls* were baptized in nearby rivers on out going tides to insure that their sins were taken away from their environs.

The Church of Christ requires a candidate for membership to do more visual seeking of Christ than the other churches do. Specific evidence of repentance by the candidate exemplified through spiritual rituals during worship service and daily life practice determines readiness for baptism and church membership.

My brief description of church worship services and membership acceptance might prompt three relevant questions from those who are curious about the essence of Gullah Spirituality:

First: Is there a specific Gullah Spirituality?
Second: Can one know Gullah Spirituality?
Thirdly: Is there tension between traditional Gullah Spirituality and modern practice of Gullah Spirituality?

I. Is there a specific Gullah Spirituality?

As I stated previously in this book Gullah Spirituality is influenced by various historic beliefs that may transcend religions and denominations. Some Gullah People on occasions combine Christian's beliefs with those of ancient Africa to satisfy their spiritual/worldly need. For example, one might combine meditation at the *mourning bench* with a *hand* (luck) from a witch doctor to relieve physical suffering or bring about needed cash. Gullah spirituality is expressed more explicitly in the title of a book recently written by Cornelia Bailey, a Sapelo Island native: "God, Dr. Buzzard and the Bolito Man". Bailey explains that the title implies that in past tradition "all three used your belief in the supernatural, dreams, signs, and magic; all three reverse your luck; and all three worked together on your behalf".

She says "Gullah people believed God's hand was in everything, but that there were certain things you did not ask God for" – you did not ask God for revenge, that was Dr. Buzzard's job; you did not ask God for money because the Christian preacher always stressed that money was the root of all evil. "You did a hard day's work to get money," Bailey states. " But you could ask God to better your condition. Then if God sent you a number and you played it with the Bolita man and got money that was okay," she said.

In past tradition, dreams were essential to Gullah Spirituality in one's Christian world too. Dreams were the media of communication between God and church leaders. Seeking and finding God through solitary meditation at a sacred location in the nearby forest, spiritually called the wilderness, and reporting nightly dreams to a spiritual leader determined one's entrance into the church membership.

In her book "Life on St. Helena Island", Isabella Glen shares that she made no progress in seeking God through dreams until a friend told her that she would never become a church member unless she told her spiritual leader that she had dreamed of catching something white. That did it she says, and she was subsequently baptized and became a member of Brick Baptist Church.

At a symposium during the Gullah celebration on Hilton Head Island, a panelist discussed how he experienced the same dream five times before his spiritual leader approved him as a worthy candidate for baptism. When the oversight committee questioned the panalist's spiritual leader why he had not approved the *Soul* for baptism when the dream was first revealed, the leader responded that he wanted to be sure. Other members of the Gullah community shared personal experiences that included the importance of faith in achieving the revealing dream. One member insisted that one's *travel* might have never ended if one lacked faith. He shared that he floundered helplessly until his spiritual leader taught him the importance of faith after which his revealing dream came quickly. Another member shared that she wore a string that contained nine knots, around her head while she was seeking. And although she could not recall the significance of the knots, the string served to distinguish her from those who were not seeking thereby insulating her from sinful distractions.

According to studies by Creel and others the above-mentioned examples of Gullah spiritual practices are in keeping with traditional African heritage of Gullah people. Supernatural causation of suffering, accidents and death under obscure circumstances " was a cure for African thought," Creel states. Magic and medicines were employed for protection and healing. West Africans have related to this writer that they too in their traditional religion believe that God lives in the forest among the dangers because He fears nothing and in order to seek him successfully, that is where one must go.

II. Can one know Gullah Spirituality?

Until the late 1960's Praise Houses were strategically located throughout the Sea Islands and other coastal communities. These were perhaps the most obvious and vibrant symbols of Gullah Spirituality. A carry-over from plantation days, these one-room whitewashed frame buildings were used for spiritual worship three times (Sunday, Tuesday, and Thursday,) weekly. The sexton ringing a cowbell 30 minutes before service began called the neighborhood to service.

Service lasted about an hour encompassing hymn, scripture, and spiritual songs and of course the prayer for *mourners*. Service usually ended with a circular shout (a religious dance with circular Afro centric rhythmic movement) and handshakes.

The Praise House experience perhaps more than any other spiritual tradition, has served to strengthen the religious belief and practice of Gullah people. In this venue, the illiterates were allowed to blunder proudly through scriptures that they partly memorized after hearing them read. Others learned how to build personal spiritual leadership capacity by exhibiting righteousness in their family and neighborhood life in order to be appointed a leadership position in the Praise House. Yet outsiders usually misinterpreted the Praise House.

When Laura Towne, a member of mainstream America culture and co-founder of Penn School, saw the shout for the first time on St. Helena Island in 1862, she described it as the most primitive ritual she had ever seen. Years later, Ms. Rosa Cooley also of mainstream America, the second principal of Penn School related that the religious practices of St. Helena Island's Gullah people "were disturbingly primitive, filled with superstition and expressed with emotion".

But for some members of the culture, the Praise House experience is an indelible memory. Whether due to nostalgia or real commitment to sacrament, Gullah people are resistant to removing Praise Houses from the neighborhood. Although there are none left standing on Hilton Head Island, there are still three on St Helena Island. Volunteers at the behest of an octogenarian, who upon returning to his birthplace after more than forty years in Philadelphia wanted to revive Praise House service, restored one of them.

Aside from the Praise House where the shout, and rhythmic hand clapping that accompany the unique coastal spiritual songs – such as "Every Time I Feel the Spirit", "Down By the River Side", and "Swing Low Sweet Chariot" are practiced, Gullah Spirituality can be known through burial practices. Virtually all family members, the church family and friends attend Gullah funerals. Past traditions called for things that the deceased desired but did not receive before dying, to be placed on the grave, or the spirit would not rest. Oftentimes the articles included food, water and lighting utensils such as oil lamps. Even the location of the cemetery helps one to know Gullah spirituality. The custom of establishing gravesites adjacent to creeks and rivers was directed by the belief of Gullah people that the spirit of the deceased would travel easily across water back to their ancestral Africa. These cemeteries have been central to the issues around privacy and access in relation to residential resort-living over the past 30 years. Fortunately, laws of most states protect cemeteries from removal without consent of families of the deceased. Otherwise the forces of Resort Development would have prevailed in having some of them moved on even destroyed.

III. Is there tension between traditional and modern practice of Gullah Spirituality?

Thus, the final question on the influence of coastal changes on Gullah Spirituality:

Is there tension between traditional practice of Gullah Spirituality and modern practice?

For the vast majority of Gullah people, official membership in the Christian church is still the official means to validating spirituality and social ability. However social and political boundaries are becoming less defined by traditional church rule than by secular rule. Unlike past traditions, today whenever both traditional Gullah church rule and secular rule are violated, secular rule supersedes church rule. In the days before coastal changes, church rule prevailed.

Some years ago, on St. Helena Island a church member consulted this writer to assist him in getting the judge to speed up the date of his trial for violating a church and secular law. He stated that he was not concerned about the secular court fine of $45.00 that he was willing and able to pay. However he was unable to deal with the fact that he had been placed on the back seat of the sanctuary. The traditional place for members who violated either church or secular rule was to place them on the rear seat of the Praise House or church. He wanted to reclaim his social status in the church.

What <u>has</u> changed is the application of rule. In past traditional Hilton Head Island for example, judges deferred all Gullah church member cases to church officials or the Gullah preferred term – The *Just Law*. In fact taking a case before the secular court by a member was considered a serious offense in traditional Gullah Spirituality. The most recent example of change in rule application was the case of a disagreement among members of a Hilton Head Gullah Baptist church that was settled by the secular court or the

Unjust law as termed by Gullahs. The rendered decision produced a split in a relative historic church and an emerging 5th Gullah Baptist church on the Island.

Although this was not the first such split, it was the first time in Island free black history that the secular court was asked to intervene in a Gullah church dispute. Other tensions are sometimes produced when Gullah members desire acceptance by the now dominant culture, resulting in a considerable degree of benign acculturation. This writer's mother resigned her resort restaurant job when her employer refused to grant her leave to attend her church on "communion Sunday" a cultural tradition that she held sacred.

And there is tension between those who are more exposed to popular culture and those who are, for a number of reasons, restricted to tradition. The gap between these two protagonists are sometimes widened by outside visitors to Gullah spiritual places, causing discomfort to the mainstream acculturated Gullah persons who assume that Gullah Spirituality is of less value than that of the new dominant culture.

In summary, Gullah Spirituality is reflective of traditional African and the subsequent adopted Christian heritage. Practiced in isolation of mainstream culture within a dominant Gullah population, the spiritual beliefs of traditional Africa dominated for more than a century in coastal communities between North Carolina and Florida.

Coastal resort residential development has produced a population shift that has subordinated the Gullah population. Regular contact between the two populations and the wider popular culture is bringing about mainstream acculturation.

Finally, Gullah people today, have access to secular rule and mainstream resources; therefore most Gullahs find this access more expedient in resolving complex societal problems. Thus there is the belief that there is lesser need for reliance on traditional spirituality in meeting worldly needs. But certain traditional spiritual practice such as the singing of old spiritual songs is being continued whenever necessary for one to retain one's place in one's adopted societal boundaries.

Christmas: Old Hilton Head Island Style

Until the late 1950's there was only one narrow paved road on the Island that began at Jenkins Island dock near the bridge, and ended at the old lighthouse at Lemington, just west of what is currently Shoppes on the Parkway. All others were winding dirt roads canopied by moss draped live oak trees or bordered by fields of grass or crops.

These dirt roads connected more than a dozen neighborhoods: Chaplin, Marshland, Gardner, Grassland, Cherry Hill, Mitchellville, Bay Gall, Squire Pope, Stoney, Jonesville, Spanish Wells, and Broad Creek. Each neighborhood contained 15-20 neatly kept little lamp lit frame houses.

Christmas truly came only **once,** a year! It was indeed a special time. Only at Christmas could we get or see toys, eat an abundance of fresh exotic fruits that were not grown on the island-- apples, bananas oranges---, and taste special sweets, while seeing certain people, like relatives from up North. They would bring special gifts for family members. I remember my sister's first return trip from New York for Christmas after being there for two years; she brought us all a little gift. But our greatest gift was her being home with us.

The Islands' separation from the mainland made it extremely difficult for Santa to reach us. But Christmas was not heavily weighted on gifts from Santa Claus. It was weighted on the belief that Christ was born on the 25th Day of December.

"When was Jesus Born" was a very popular folk song during Christmas time. It seemed people sang that rather amusing tune wherever more than two gathered:

When was Jesus born?
Chorus:
The last month of the year
(Repeat trice)
Was it January?
Chorus:
No! No!
February?
No! No!!
March, April, May?
No! No! No!
June, July, August
September, October, No-vember,
The twenty- fifth day of De-cem-ber

The last month of the year!

And so beginning in the spring we prepared for Christmas every season of the year. Every significant effort was made with Christmas in mind. Around April Christmas turkeys began hatching to be sold at Savannah's markets in December to get cash for toys, clothing, etc. As a young boy I had the responsibility of caring for as many as a dozen little turkeys from the time they hatched until they were taken to market.

My job was to prepare their feed every morning and afternoon. Between feedings they were allowed to roam the fields to feed on wild plants and insects. Then I had to find them in the late afternoons and shoo them back to the hen house for a feeding before bedtime. Shooing turkeys is an extremely challenging task because they do not stay together very long before suddenly dispersing in all directions for no apparent reason. Their crazy action would wear my patience and bring me close to critically hurting them. Turkeys are very delicate and I learned early that my life was closely connected to theirs. Mother constantly reminded me of the grave consequence I would face if a turkey had died as a result of my negligence. In fact she would imply that the treatment would be reciprocal. It was very clear that she counted early the dividends each turkey would bring to help her fulfill our Christmas wishes.

Spring was the time when Christmas Savings Clubs were organized so that cash would be available for Christmas. It was when blackberries, mulberries,
and plums were harvested from which wines were made for Christmas.

In the summer peaches and sugar figs and pears were preserved to serve for Christmas deserts. And okra, tomatoes, beans and other vegetables were preserved for use at Christmas meals.

In the Fall there were an abundance of nuts and we enthusiastically gathered pecans, walnuts and wild chinquapin for Christmas. And after we harvested corn we took bushels to one of several grits mills to be grounded into grits for winter meals. And we would begin Catalog shopping at Sears, Montgomery Ward and Walter Fields and orders would come cash on delivery (C. O. D.).

Then came November and December and people repaired their houses as needed, added a room, painted furniture, or improved their yard fences. "Christmas Fish" were caught and preserved. "Christmas Fog" would evolve and pose a constant travel hazard on the waterways. Sometimes Captains would get temporarily disoriented or grounded on banks before reaching Savannah.

Houses were painted gay colors:

Blue with White trim
White and blue trim
Yellowish black trim
Gray with White, floors were stained, etc.

My mother's favorite color was blue and she always had us paint the house royal blue trimmed with bright white each year before Christmas. And since the Christmas holiday lasted for an entire week, every household hauled several wagonloads of firewood and we children would chop enough in stove length to last the week.

Then came Christmas Eve and by now the Christmas Spirit would be exuberating. Every neighborhood conducted Praise House Services until Christmas Arrived. Santa would leave his reindeer in Savannah and load his gifts on the Sailboats: The "Waldorf", the "River Queen", the "Wish away", the "Rome" or some other. When gasoline engines became available Santa brought his gifts on the "Edgar Hurst", the "Alligator" or the "Vernon". We decorated our Christmas trees with such natural ornaments as Spanish Moss, holly bushes, and pine cones. Families cooked all night as children went to bed early. Parents and children, who were too old for Santa's gifts, prepared Christmas meats, such as, fresh pork, raccoon, rabbit and turkey.

On Christmas Day everyone woke up Merry! Red wagons, dolls, key wound toys, battery run trains and needed clothing would clutter the tree. At our house my mother usually prepared early morning breakfast: grits and Seafood --- fish, shrimp or oysters ---- with browned onion gravy served with her deliciously baked biscuits and hot cocoa.

Beginning soon after breakfast, men and children separately would visit every house in the neighborhood. The children would be served fresh nuts, candy, and fruits such as - apples, oranges, and grapes, and a glass of soft drink. The men would be served portions of meat, veggies, starches, desserts, or a full meal --- rice dishes, baked raccoon, potato salad, turkey, roast pork, potato pie, turnip greens, pumpkin pie, etc. And fine wines were made from the berries of the Spring. During their visit the men would gather around the table and sing old spirituals and tell folk tales.

In the Marshland neighborhood, the men mainly from that end of the Island held an annual Christmas Day horse race. A portion of Marshland road from "Big Gate" now Mathews Drive one mile southwestward was the designated track. Legend has it that a horse named “Nail Um” was usually one of the most favored to win.

On the day after Christmas women would make house to house visits for delicious foods and home-made spirits, following the same routine as the men did the previous day except they sang old spirituals as they walked. Their harmonious voices could be heard from a considerable distance in the still winter ambience of the Island. And whenever a member of the group became intoxicated and lost control of her posture, the leader applied firm chops across the hips with a switch from the forest. This seemingly brought immediate compliance from the victim and the others would invoke a degree of discipline in their intake of “refreshments” from the tables.

Eventually Christmas would come to a regretful end just before New Years arrived, with its own special treats, and everyone would soon begin preparing for the next Christmas.

Penn Center Heritage Days Celebration Parade

The Penn Center Heritage Days Celebration Parade has evolved into one of the most popular Gullah cultural art forms of the Southeastern United States. It is the most popular attraction of the nationally known Penn Center Heritage Days Celebration that is held on St. Helena Island, SC every November. In fact, the growth of the entire celebration is largely attributable to the parade.

Since 1981, the celebration has been held annually every November beginning on the second Thursday afternoon and ending the following Sunday after church services. Its purpose is to exhibit Gullah customs, traditions and art forms, and the history of Penn Center, widely known as one of the vanguards in academic teachings for the newly freed during the American Civil War.

In 1985 the celebration planners initiated a community-based parade to climax the event. In addition to giving the audience a reference for the final day's beginning, the parade reflects the culture of the region. Participating units perform in accordance with Gullah cultural traditions, displaying art forms ranging from that which depicts the role of community elders to "jump (picnic) band" music.

Participating groups include fraternities and sororities, farmers groups, daycare centers, the military bands, fire departments and others, resulting in a parade of about 100 units. Beginning at the St. Helena Elementary School on U.S. Highway 21 East (the only route to and from the main land) West to Martin Luther King Drive, then South to Penn Center Historical Landmark District.

To insure that the parade projects a composite scene, the theme of the Heritage Celebration is embraced as the official guiding topic by which floats and other expressive units are decorated. The original red and white Penn School colors are used as the base with which all others are blended. Over the years themes have ranged from the Penn School historic graduation mottos to recently composed themes of the Heritage Celebration Community planning committee. These themes have included, "Bend to the Oar, although the Tide Be Against You," "A History of Pride," "Continuing A Legacy," "The Sea Islands: A Common History, A Common Culture," and "The African American Family: Preserving Leadership Through Cultural Involvement."

Units are strategically organized in order of cultural importance: The Parade marshals who are selected from among the Islands' eldest women and men, representing wisdom, endurance, vision and courage are the first in line. Life long residents of the Sea Islands, they are chosen after careful research and committee verification. These marshals have ranged in ages from 90 to 101 years. Next, colors are borne by students from JROTC programs in local schools. Proudly stepping between walls of spectators formed along the highway, each of three students bears the flag of the United States, the State of South Carolina and Penn Center. These students represent youth, leadership and disciplined behavior. In 2001, elementary school students began a tradition of artfully displaying forty West African and Caribbean nation flags, representing those regions from which Gullahs came to the Sea Islands.

High schools, community and military marching bands, church gospel choirs and children and youth stepping groups of churches and Greek letter organizations portray music and movements of the culture. Theme floats depict the theme of the year and specific features of the Gullah culture. For example, in 2001 the theme "Bound

Together by Common Threads" evoked floats with quilts, baskets and family and community members. Other floats depict food gathering on sea and land; a bateau with fish net and seafood, trimmed with salt marsh and sea weed; a farm tractor (at least one antique) decorated with farm produce bordered with Spanish moss, palmetto and other native plants; and Penn school education--- a classroom set up with young children sitting studiously at wooden desks and a black board commemorating and stressing the importance of education today.

Units demonstrating food-gathering traditions trigger memories of casting handmade fish and shrimp nets in local creeks from bateaux made by local Gullah craftsmen. The antique farm tractors and farm produce reflect traditional farm practices that have been gradually changing since the early 1940's when some Gullah families began buying tractors. Mechanism has replaced family farm workers in producing the traditional crops of rice, water melon, sugar cane, sweet potatoes, collard greens, etc., that are bought on site during the celebration.

Each year a prize is awarded for the unit best portraying the Heritage Day Celebration theme.

Float in 2000 Heritage Days Parade depicting Togetherness
Photo Courtesy of Walter Mack

Soon after sunrise on the morning of the parade several thousand spectators begin gathering along the narrow parade route to secure the perfect spot from which to get a satisfying view of the performance.

Although many in the audience come from as far away as the Northeast and the Midwest, most are Gullah people from the South Carolina and Georgia Sea Islands. By the time the units transcend its view, the audience is poised with anticipation and eager to exude enthusiastic prideful applause. The colorful crowds perched under trees of live oak evergreens, fall color of sweet gums, loblolly pines, occasional maple, magnolia and the prevalent Palmetto tree make an extraordinary picturesque Sea Island landscape.

Parade audience along Martin Luther King Drive
Photo Courtesy of Walter Mack

The Parade begins promptly with the color guards of the high school JROTC students carrying the flags of the United States, the state of South Carolina (boasting a solid blue with a crescent moon in the upper right and a Palmetto tree in the center); and the Penn Center flag (a solid red with a large white "P" in the center). Moving in unified steps behind a police patrol car, they set the pace for following units.

Paris Island Marines Band follows the color guard. A very stout professional band that plays the usual patriotic songs, "This is my Country", "America the Beautiful", etc. and the ballads of the Marine Corps, the band members exemplify toughness and discipline.

Next in line are the Grand Marshals. Two of the eldest males and females of the immediate islands are chauffeured in antique cars characteristic of their distinguished age treating the audience with a sense of community memory of time past.

The Penn Center Trustee Board Chairman, the Executive Director and the Heritage Days Celebration

Planning Committee Chairman follow, just ahead of the "flags of the Gullah people." These flags represent each of the --- nations including Sierra Leone, Senegal, Nigeria, Angola and other West African nations from which Gullah ancestors came during slavery. Then one of the high school marching bands units exercise its talents to inspire the other units and maintain cultural form attraction.

Students carrying "flags of the Gullah People"
Photo Courtesy of Walter Mack

Several units of vehicles and individuals representing organizations such as, the NAACP, and churches are followed by one of the floats depicting a cultural feature, i.e., food gathering. A marching band follows these units. Most of the band members are students from Gullah families. Again the vibrant sound of a familiar tune and the vigorous movement of youth attract the audience. This alternation of marching bands in the midst of walking and vehicular units of day care centers and fraternal organizations continue until the parade ends.

Beaufort High School Band of which most members are St. Helena Islanders
Photo Courtesy of Walter Mack

After the usual unhurried procession of several vehicles the parade is interspersed with a unit of steppers who perform by marching in quick steps, hand-clapping and unified body twists while chanting composed verses. Stepping and stomping originated when African American Greek letter fraternity brothers returned from World War II. Other influences come from marching African American Armies of antiquity; the Nubian Warriors, Zulu Legions, etc. Some steppers replaced the doo-woop sound and African movements by the 1960's incorporating the South African "boot dance." (Stepping, Greek Letter Organizations)

Elementary School Student Steppers
Photo Courtesy of Walter Mack

The audience of children and adults passionately displays enthusiasm for the duration of the parade. Its impression is dispersed through cheering; pleasing names calls and proud smiles. The fourth stanza of Paul Laurence Dunbar's poem "The Colored Band" very closely describes the reaction one may sense in the audience's reaction to the Penn Center Heritage Days Celebration Parade:

W'en de colo'ed ban'came ma'ch.
in'down de street
you kin hyeah de ladies all arroam'
repeat:
"Aint day handsom? Aint
day gran'?
Ain't dey splendid? Goodness,
Lan'!
W'y dey's pu'fect f'om dey fo'-
heads to dy feet!
An'sich steppin'to de music down

de line,
"T'aint de music by itself ldat meks
it fine
Hit's de walkin', step by step,
An de keepin'time wid "Hep"
Dat it mek a commn ditty soon'
Divine.(Dunbar, 16)

Heritage Days Marching Band, November 1999
Photo courtesy Penn Center, Inc.

The entire Penn Heritage parade is indeed like the "colored band". The sixty or more units harmonizing in steps, rhythms, colors, sounds and body language is like railroad cars moving down the narrow U.S. Highway 21, making a sharp left turn onto Martin Luther King Drive after nearly a mile, then climaxing at live oak canopied Penn Center Historic Landmark District (the station).

The summit of the parade is characterized by two obvious occurrences: 1) The otherwise flat Martin Luther King Drive suddenly elevates nearly ten feet immediately after it bridges across a salt marsh creek. This ridge comprises the entire Penn Center Historic District, which is ideal for its majestic live oak trees. 2) The judges' stand is located in the vicinity (about a hundred yards before the end of the parade) where competing parade units give special performances in pursuit of the offered prizes.

Antique tractor pulling float
Photo Courtesy of Walter Mack

Under the canopy of moss-draped live oaks on the narrow paved black-top Martin Luther King Drive, the floats crawl at a Low Country coota's (Gullah word for turtle) pace, while six judges give their undivided attentive gazes. Roosted on the bluff above the highway they rate each competitor on neatness and appearance, creativity and originality, multi-generational, and theme appropriateness. (Appendix 2)

At the same location all bands, except the military band, give performances of their music and movements. These bands may render previously rehearsed historical musical numbers that include jazz, blues, or contemporary musical numbers that include the St. Louis blues, 1960's tunes, such as "the Motown Sound" and most recent Hip Hop tunes. Their movements, consistent with the music and tunes, include the Cha Cha, the Bump, some "homemade" or improvised movements, etc. The bands are judged on musicianship, marching style, creativity and originality.

These performances prepare the cheering crowds for a day of fine Gullah cuisine, a variety of Gullah Cultural forms from center stage whence the prizes are awarded.

Drummers preceding " The Gullah Queen"
Photo Courtesy of Walter Mack

At this point the Heritage Days parade climaxes as an outstanding Gullah cultural art form. It embodies the Gullah culture in a convincing art form – the family depicted by the elders and youth, food ways (rice, sweet potatoes, etc) spirituality (Gospel choirs), visual art (baskets), performance art (bands and music) are all presented artfully in an hour and a half to a diverse and appreciative audience. The Penn Center Heritage Days Celebration Parade is indeed a cultural art form where one has the rare opportunity to thoroughly immerse oneself in the Gullah culture.

Epilogue

Yes You Can Go Home Again:

A Visit of Fifteen Sea Islanders to Sierra Leone, West Africa

To my knowledge there has not yet been determined any specific place in West Africa to assign the entire origin of the Gullah Culture. However, evidence of cultural linkages and language has been identified in a number of present day West African Nations. I was privileged to visit with fourteen other Sea Islanders, one of the nations, Sierra Leone. I am pleased to share this experience with you here in furthering the understanding of Gullah Cultural Legacies.

Dr. Joseph Holloway had contacted me through a mutual friend, Dr. Herman Blake of John's Island origin. When Joe arrived, I reluctantly spent a good deal of time listening to his claim that we in the Sea Islands had retained more "Africanisms" than most African Americans. He insisted that our language was the most permanent link to our West African origin. Eventually, I was totally convinced that Gullah is indeed related to West African languages when Joe arranged for me to meet with two wonderful missionaries, Claude and Pat Sharpe, who had been translating the Bible into Gullah. They had been working on the project for several years in the Daufuskie Island -St. Helena Island area. Their scholarly explanation of the similarities in our language to that of West African's was most intriguing.

About a year later I received a letter from Joseph Opala, who had remained in his host country, Sierra Leone, after serving as a Peace Corps volunteer. He expressed a great deal of enthusiasm for the work he had begun on the connection between African Americans and West Africans. A day after New Years in 1987, Joe came to Penn Center and gave an enthusiastic lecture to more than 100 Islanders and friends. He explained the results of his research on the slave trade involving Sierra Leoneans. He had further substantiated the findings of other scholars that many Africans had been imported to South Carolina from Sierra Leone because of their knowledge in rice agricultural technology. He had found that in addition to the language (Gullah), we had retained many recipes that Sierra Leoneans still use. Most of those present left proud and excited that someone had finally explained the importance of Gullah. Another surprising result of his research was the fact that enslaved Africans of the Sea Islands had run away to Florida and joined forces with the Seminoles against the United States government. Thus, the reasons for the Black Seminoles of Oklahoma who still speak Gullah.

Then in 1988, true to the promise that he had conveyed through Joe Opala, the president of Sierra Leone, His Excellency Dr. Joseph Momoh, visited Penn Center while in the US to visit President Reagan. The president of South Carolina State College, Dr. Al Smith, coordinated his trip to the area. When I greeted His Excellency and his entourage in Gullah, "We Glad fa see oonah,"(we're glad to see you) they obviously felt that they had found their long lost relatives who had perhaps left Sierra Leone many years before.

In November of 1989, South Carolina State College completed arrangements for a delegation of Gullahs from Oklahoma and the Sea Islands of Georgia and South Carolina to "go home": Cornelia Bailey and Loretta Sam of Sapelo Island and Darien, Georgia; Doug and Frankie Quimby of St. Simons Island, Georgia; Myrtle Glascoe of the Avery Research Center at the College of Charleston and Elaine Jenkins of Johns Island, South Carolina; Black Seminole twin cujoe brothers, Lawrence and Lance, and Lance's wife Freddie, of Oklahoma City, Oklahoma; and Earnestine Atkins and me of the St. Helena Island area. Senator John Matthews of Orangeburg, SC, and Senator Arnett Girardeau of Jacksonville, FL, represented their respective states' government; and

Dr. Alpha Bah, a Sierra Leonean history professor at the College of Charleston, served as our very able escort.

A little more than 30 hours after we left Savannah International Airport we arrived at the Longe airport, across the bay from Freetown, Sierra Leone. As we disembarked, the plane, nearly a thousand people from various villages greeted us. Their dances, smiles and rhythmic drumming made us know that we had come home. Dr. A.K. Turay, Joe Opala, Key cabinet ministers and our own South Carolina Educational Television people, Tim Carrier and Dolano Boulware, greeted us.

The week went fast as we traveled through the country to the waves, smiles and banners that read "Welcome our Gullah Brothers and Sisters from South Carolina and Georgia, We Glad Fa See Oonah."It did not matter that the French airline had misplaced our luggage, for President Momoh had us all fitted with beautiful African outfits at a downtown boutique. During the cultural affair that followed an elaborate dinner hosted by His Excellency at the state house that Tuesday evening, one speaker said it was appropriate that His Excellency clothed us, since our ancestors had left years ago stripped of their clothing.

The people of Sierra Leone are terrific! Like Gullah communities in South Carolina and Georgia, they are proud, friendly and industrious. We saw their smiles, spoke to them in our common language — Gullah and Krio, which are very similar — and observed their entrepreneurship at King Jimmy's market, where hundreds bought and sold vegetables, fish, clothing, baskets and other products. We shared their delicious rice dishes, fish and vegetables at every meal. Not surprising anymore, their food and recipes were very much like ours in the Gullah community.

We met hundreds of men, women and children as we toured the country, and we saw the place whence our ancestors left-Bunce Island. The jetty from which they had boarded the ship nearly 300 years before was where we landed. The chief of the nearby village and his entourage sacredly performed the libation ceremony. This was perhaps the most emotional moment of our visit. We proceeded to examine the entire island, including the cannons used to prevent theft of the captured Africans before being shipped away. How could that have been, I kept wondering. With a sense of satisfaction that I was standing where many began their dreadful trek to a system of slavery, I could not hold back the tears.

The beaches were beautiful — like ours in the Sea Islands, except they are open to everyone, just like ours once were — open to everyone to fish, to play, to walk. Free.

And Tiama Village, sixty miles south of Freetown could be any community of Gullah families in the Sea Islands. "We glad fa see oonah" was not only on a sign like we had seen throughout the country, but on the face of each person. The children had stayed out of school to see us and the adults were tearfully glad "fa see we." They kept us all day, showing us their rice fields, their dances, their weaving work and feeding us well. What a people! What colorful masks and rhythmic movements! How beautiful! And oh how much we danced to the drums!

On the final day we visited the Regent Community, where we went to church. Africans who had returned from slavery established this community. They sang our songs: "Steal Away," "Swing Low Sweet Chariot," and "Old Time Religion." The minister admonished African in the Diaspora against complacency. In essence, he reiterated, "Freedom is not Free."

Many people had helped to make our trip enjoyable. To mention a few, Arthur Lewis and his company had paid for Ernestine's and my tickets. Tom Stewart of South Carolina State College had worked tirelessly to coordinate the trip. My Board of Trustees had permitted me to go. The U.S. Embassy on Sierra Leone was just wonderfully helpful. And the People of Sierra Leone!

What had this entire story mean? I could never tell you in words. Upon my return from Sierra Leone, a member of our staff at Penn Center exclaimed, "Mr. Campbell appears taller." At six foot four, one would think that is impossible—but I had, indeed, grown. I had grown not in physical stature, but truly in self-pride. Yes, you can now call me "Gullah," for I have gone home again.

Suggested Key Strategies for Cultural Preservation

In these days of cybernation, global emigration and outer space exploration, the intricate undertaking of retaining cultural integrity is ubiquitous. Surely the integrity of the Gullah Culture is being affected by these factors and like other affected cultures these factors must be modified in order to preserve cultural integrity. In essence these popular cultural elements could be used in concert with traditional cultural assets in advancing indigenous cultural integrity.

It is commonly accepted that the Gullah culture is geographically contained primarily between Jacksonville, North Carolina and Jacksonville, Florida. Based on the 2000 U.S. census nearly one million African Americans are residents of this coastal region (designated for land sale to former slaves in 1862 from the Atlantic Ocean to fifty miles inland). Of course, the dominant factor affecting Gullah cultural integrity is the immigration of Americans of European ancestry who are attracted by the relatively mild climate, and an aesthetically beautiful resort environment.

To a lesser degree these immigrants, most of whom represent mainstream American culture, are also attracted by the unique Gullah cultural heritage. This attraction is attributable to the immigrants' intellectual curiosity for history, traditional Gullah arts and food ways that could direct a mutually rewarding relationship between the binyas's and the comya's. This relationship is critical to preserving cultural assets that would reduce friction between the two groups and promote a sustainable, livable region.

Throughout my work in the Gullah Culture over a number of years, I have learned valuable lessons that perhaps could be transformed into strategies for preserving Gullah as well as other cultures. I offer these suggestions here upon which you, the reader of this book, could consider involving families, communities and public policy makers to act.

1. Family

- Preserve family land for residential use and economic ventures. Encourage family villages, and long –term leasing in preventing transfer of family land ownership.
- Conduct regular family gatherings and extended family reunions to maintain connection of kinship and family assets through learning workshops and genealogy estate planning.
- Instill traditional family principles of work ethics, academicism, education, morals and behavior in children.
- Teach traditional art forms to children.
- Prepare traditional recipes regularly for family meals.
- Maintain residential and surrounding property in good repair and decently landscaped.
- Keep property tax current.
- Organize family members for the purpose of investing in land and other property.

2. Community

- Define Gullah cultural assets including art forms, food ways, and educational, spiritual and cultural institutions in sustaining communities.
- Organize and sponsor regular celebrations of cultural traditions, and art forms and food ways.
- Maintain vibrant institutions of education, spirituality and language and cultural arts.
- Organize and maintain property owners associations to regularly address issues and problems of common interest, including keeping the neighborhood pleasantly landscaped.
- Provide opportunities for schooling public policy makers (i.e. county council, town councils, planning boards, etc.) and community members on Gullah cultural preservation issues.
- Promote Gullah culturally based economic ventures, such as restaurants, art galleries, etc.
- Conduct community land use planning sessions in collaboration with public policy making bodies when appropriate.
- Organize and maintain an active Community Land Trust to acquire land for community use.

3. Public Policy Members

- Recognize the Gullah culture as one that contains unique assets that promote sound family principles and livable communities.
- Promote opportunities for members to learn lessons on specific cultural features.

- Develop political and physical infrastructure that allows and encourages Gullah participation in the democratic and economic development process, i.e. create voting and public service districts, etc.

- In collaboration with financial institutions and members of the culture, develop and implement strategic financing plans for enhancing economic and community development.

- Devise a system that would allow property owners to pay annual property taxes in installments. This would lessen the burden that one-time payments present on the family budget and reduce the number of parcels lost for delinquent taxes.

SUGGESTED READING ON GULLAH PEOPLE OF THE SEA ISLANDS AND THE PENN SCHOOL/CENTER

Over the years persons of varying disciplines and interests in history and culture have made serious attempts to unravel the mystique of Gullah culture. These endeavors have resulted in publication of a substantial number of books, documentary films and commentaries. The following abbreviated list of publications are among secondary references that may further your understanding of the Gullah cultural heritage. However this list should not be construed as an inclusive list of publications and sources for studying the Gullah culture.

Gullah Life

Ashe, Jeane Moutoussamy, Daufuskie Island: A Photographic Essay. Columbia: University of South Carolina Press, 1982.

Bailey, Cornelia Walker, God, Dr. Buzzard and The Bolito Man. New York: Doubleday.

Black, J. Gary, My Friend the Gullah. Columbia: The R.L. Bryan, 1974.

Campbell, Emory S., Gullah Cultural Legacies. Hilton Head Island: Gullah Heritage Consulting Services (GCHCS), LLC.

Daise, Ronald, Reminiscences of Sea Island Heritage. Orangeburg: Sandlapper Publishing, Inc., 1986.

Hilton, Mary Kindall, Old Homes and Churches of Beaufort County, South Carolina. Columbia: State Printing Company, 1970.

Johnson, Guion Griffin, A Social History of the Sea Islands with Special Reference to St. Helena Island, South Carolina. Chapel Hill: University of North Carolina Press, 1930.

Jones-Jackson, Patricia, When Roots Die. University of Georgia Press. 1987.

Joyner, Charles, Down By the Riverside. Chicago: University of Illinois Press.

Joyner, Charles, Shared Traditions. Chicago: University of Illinois Press.

Krull, Kathleen. Bridges To Change: How Kids Live on a South Carolina Sea Island. Lodestar Books, New York, 1995.

Gullah Spirituality

Ballenta, Nicholas George Jullus, St. Helena Island Spirituals, Recorded and Transcribed at Penn Normal, Industrial and Agricultural School. New York: W.W. Norton and Company.

Creel, Margaret Washington, A Peculiar People: Slave Religion and Community – Culture Among the Gullahs. New York: New York University Press, 1988.

Parrish, Lydia. Slave Songs of the Georgia Sea Islands. University of Georgia Press, Athens 1992.

Gullah Speech/folklore

Daise, Ronald, Little Muddy Waters, G.O.G. Enterprises, Beaufort, South Carolina,1997.

Geraty, Virgina. Gullah Fuh Oonuh: A Guide to the Gullah Language. Sanlapper Publishing Company, Orangeburg, South Carolina, 1997.

Jones, Charles Colcock, Gullah Folktales from the Gullah Coast. University of Georgia Press, Athens, Ga. 2000.

Stoddard, Albert. Gullah Animal Tales. Push Button Publishing Company. Hilton Head Island, South Carolina.1996.

Turner, Lorenzo D. Africanisms in the Gullah Dialect. Ann Arbor: The University of Michigan Press, 1949.

Gullah Art

Green, Jonathan, Gullah Images: The Art of Jonathan Green, University of South Carolina Press Columbia. 1996.

Rosengarten, Dale. Sea (Sweet) Grass Baskets of South Carolina Low Country. McKissick Museum, University of South Carolina, Columbia, South Carolina, 1986.

Gullah Foodways

Grosvenor, Vertamae, Vertamae Cooks in America's Family Kitchen, KQED Books, San Francisco, Ca. 1996.

Robinson, Sallie Ann, Gullah Home Cooking the Daufuskie Way. University of North Carolina Press. 2003.

Gantt, Jesse Edward and Gerald, Veronica Davis, The Ultimate Gullah Cookbook. Sands Publishing, Beaufort, SC. 2002.

Education

Billington, Ray Allen, The Journal of Charlotte L. Forten: A Free Negro in the Slave Era. New York: W.W. Norton and Company.

Cooley, Roosa, Homes of the Free. New York: New Republic, Inc.

Dabbs, Edith M., Faces of An Island. The Leigh Richmond Miner's Photographs. Columbia: The R.L. Bryan, 1970.

Holland, Rupert Sargent, Letters and Diary of Laura M. Towne: Written from the Sea Islands of South Carolina 1862-1884. New York: Negro University Press, 1912.

Jacoway, Elizabeth, Yankee Missionary in the South: The Penn School Experiment. Baton Rouge: Louisiana State University Press, 1980.

Longwood, Polly, I Charlotte Forten, Black and Free. New York: Thomas Y. Crowell Company, 1920.

History

Carney, Judith. Black Rice: Cultivation The African Origin of Rice in the Americas. Harvard University Press. Cambridge, Ma. 2001..

Gordon, Asa H., Sketches of Negro Life and History in South Carolina. Columbia: University of South Carolina Press, 1970.

Littlefield, Daniel. Rice and Slaves: Ethnicity and the Slave Trade in Colonial South Carolina. Louisiana State Press. Baton Rouge.1981.

Newby, I.A., Black Carolinians: A History of Blacks in South Carolina from 1865 to 1968. Columbia: University of South Carolina Press, 1973.

Pollitzer, William S., The Gullah People and Their African Heritage. Atlanta, Ga.: The university of Georgia Press.

Smith, Julia Floyd, Slavery and Rice Culture in Low Country Georgia 1750-1860. Knoxville: The University of Tennessee Press, 1985.

Sterling, Dorothy, Captain of the Planter: The Story of Robert Smalls. Garden City: Doubleday and Company, 1958.

Rose, Willie Lee, Rehearsal for Reconstruction: The Port Royal Experiment. Indianapolis: The Bobbs-Merrill Company, 1964.

Thornbough, Margaret, Black Reconstructionist. Englewood Cliffs: Prentice-Hall, 1972.

Tindall, George Brown, South Carolina Negroes: 1877-1900. Columbia: University of South Carolina Press, 1952.

Twining Mary A. and Keith Baird. Sea Island Roots: The African Presence in the Carolinas and Georgia. Africa World Press, Inc. 1991.

Wood, Peter, Black Majority: Negroes in Colonial South Carolina 167- through the Stone Rebellion.

PAMPHLETS AND ARTICLES

1. Blockson, Charles L. "*Sea Change in the Sea Islands, No Where To Lay Down Weary Head.*" National Geographic, December 1987, pp. 735-763.

2. Chepesiuk, Ron. *"The Gullah Bible: A Link Between Past and Future."* American Visions, June 1988, pp. 32-36.

3. Sea Grass Baskets of the South Carolina Low Country: Row Upon Row. Columbia, S.C. McKissick Museum, 1987.

4. The Gullah: Rice, Slavery and the Sierra Leone-American Connection. Joe Opala.

FILMS AND VIDEO

1. Daughters of the Dust: Commercial Market.

2. Family Across the Sea: S.C. ETV

3. God's Gonna Trouble the Water: S.C. ETV

4. Charlotte Forten's Mission: PBS

5. The Language You Cry In: PBS

6. Where Roots Endure: PBS

Acknowledgements

My sincerest thanks go to my eleven siblings who continuously tell stories of our childhood experiences during our regular family gatherings. My memory is always refreshed during these gatherings as we recollect wonderful Gullah cultural legacies. Although we all grew up Gullah, the differences in our ages and diversity in experiences (four of us were reared by our grandparents) gives me a superbly rich reservoir of legends. I shall present them here chronologically with their basket or nickname: George (Tackle), the eldest who was raised by our maternal grandparents, gave me my earliest experiences in the waterways and forests while gathering seafood and firewood, Carol (Dooley) my eldest sister who was our caretaker when our parents were away, Reggie Mae (Regina) (Bones) who like George, was raised by our maternal Grandparents and remembers stories she learned from them, Hattie (Hat) who was raised by our paternal grandparents often relates her memories of their folklores, Herbert (Timer) who always hanged around the elders knows how to embellish stories to keep one's attention, David who can recall some of the rarest legacies of his fishing trips with grandmother Big Rose that pleasantly jogs my memory, Leroy (Bon) deceased, was also raised by our maternal grandparents helped me to appreciate our grandfather's fish net knitting skills. He was the only one among us who learned the art; Irvin (Dewey) the only pre term birth among us is a grateful beneficiary of new born folk medicine; Melvin (Buddy) the only career School Teacher of our generation after six school teachers in previous generations. He is astute at distinguishing between tradition and modernity; Morris (Battey) the first among us to break the color/cultural barrier of formal schooling when he was among the first Black students to attend a previously all White school in the 1960's;

Ben who lived with our parents for the longest period there by perhaps more refreshed with memories of their sharing.

And I appreciate very much my closeness with two special first cousins, Clarence (Say Hey, Fatty) and Sol (June) for their timely recollections and my brothers and sisters in-law for their interest in our stories.

I am truly grateful for my academic friends; Dr. J Herman Blake, Dr. Joseph Hollaway, Joseph Opala, Virginia Garaty, Pat and Claude Sharpe and the Gullah Bible translation team all whom inspired me to give serious attention to these Gullah cultural legacies.

A special thanks to Vertamae Grosvenor for exposing the world to Gullah cooking and to my editor, Tamara Holmes, for untangling my Gullah grammar to English grammar.

Finally, I owe a great debt of gratitude to my good friend Thomas C. Barnwell, Jr., who was the first to provide me the opportunity, in my professional life, to work closely with my fellow Gullah people.

One of the last dirt roads left on Hilton Head Island.

Index

About the Author

Emory Shaw Campbell is an example of a native son who left his early environment and later returned not only as a leader but also as a visionary and proponent of constructive programs and policies. He was born in 1941 on Hilton Head, one of many islands off the coast of South Carolina and Georgia. Because of the isolation of these sea islands, the inhabitants were able to maintain their unique culture and language patterns. From his parents and grandparents, Campbell learned the importance of education, family and community. His parents and paternal grandparents were all teachers.

When Campbell was young, high schools did not exist on Hilton Head Island. However, he was able to attend high school in the town of Bluffton, which had been recently linked to Hilton Head via a bridge. He studied at the segregated Michael C. Riley High School, graduating in 1960 as class valedictorian. Enrolling at Savannah State College, Campbell showed his determination to succeed by making a forty mile a day commute, often hitchhiking in order to attend classes. In 1965, he earned his Bachelor of Science degree in biology.

Joining the microbiology department at the Harvard School of Public Health, he researched by day and tutored students in the evening. Campbell's concern for the future of the sea islands became apparent as he continued his education. Observing that "the urgent need on South Carolina's sea islands was skills among the indigenous citizens to address issues related to their environment and cultural heritage," Campbell was true to his convictions. After completing his M.A. at Tufts University in Boston, he returned to South Carolina to work at the Comprehensive Health Agency for Beaufort and Jasper counties. For almost ten years, he traveled throughout the sea islands, addressing environmental issues which affected the daily lives of the islands' people. His goal was to inform and discuss methods of preserving and enhancing the unique and rich Gullah heritage in the face of rapid development on the islands.

In 1980, Campbell took a step closer to his goal by becoming the executive director of Penn Center on St. Helena Island. (Founded in 1862, during the Civil War, by northern missionaries and teachers to help freed slaves as part of the Port Royal experiment, Penn Center became the first industrial training school for African-Americans in the United States.) He vigorously embarked on a program to revive the center's historical significance and to preserve the culture of the sea islands. To help achieve this, he organized the now nationally recognized Penn Center Heritage Days Celebration. He also revised the family farm program and expanded the museum program to assist writers, film makers and authors, among them Jeanne Moutoussamy-Ashe, Patricia Jones-Jackson and VertaMae Grosvenor.

Campbell has appeared in many documentaries, news magazines, films and radio and television programs, including 60 Minutes, the Today Show and a PBS special, Family Across The Sea. The contribution that Emory Shaw Campbell has made to the cultural heritage of South Carolina is enormous. He and his family live on Hilton Head Island, where he grew up and developed his love of the sea islands. Among his honors is a Doctorate in Humane Letters from Bank Street College, New York.

Campbell is co-founder of the Gullah Heritage Trail Tours, a family business that guides travelers in learning about traditional Gullah neighborhoods and environs on Hilton Head and vicinal Islands.

77935